Books by

SALLY CARRIGHAR

ICEBOUND SUMMER (1953)

ONE DAY AT TETON MARSH (1947)

ONE DAY ON BEETLE ROCK (1944)

These are Borzoi Books

Published by ALFRED A. KNOPF *in New York*

ICEBOUND SUMMER

Icebound Summer

SALLY CARRIGHAR

Illustrations by HENRY B. KANE

1954

NEW YORK : ALFRED A. KNOPF

L. C. catalog card number: 52–12184

THIS IS A BORZOI BOOK,
PUBLISHED BY ALFRED A. KNOPF, INC.

PUBLISHED JULY 20, 1953
SECOND PRINTING, AUGUST 1953
THIRD PRINTING, NOVEMBER 1953
FOURTH PRINTING, JANUARY 1954

TO MY MOTHER

Introduction

DURING THE WINTER the white wilderness of the North seems like a planet where life has not yet appeared. It has the same prehistoric elements: snow and ice, and the sky. For hundreds of miles nothing else can be glimpsed.

The frozen sea may be level or heaved into ridges. In either case it is vastly wide. Snow covers it, and across most of the white expanse nothing has fallen, no dust, and no foot or paw. No voice is heard there. The low, grinding crunch of the ice pack itself, if it shifts on the tide, is the only sound. The sky, with no smoke rising into it, has a pure, almost glittering clarity. It is empty of birds. The blaze of the Northern stars, and the moon, and the sun when the dark months are past, make their slow progress over it; otherwise nothing moves in this dome except winds and clouds.

When the snow is on it, much of the arctic land, as well as the silent and motionless sea, might belong to the earth's beginnings. And as the snow disappears, the tundra is found to be clothed chiefly with primitive mosses and lichens. In a scene like this the memory of civilized comforts is the fantastic thought. Gadgets: they are the strangeness. City, state, and national borders seem nearly as temporary as lines drawn on the snow. The boundaries one is more aware of are the perimeters of the planet, the constellations, and galaxies. One discovers infinity, not as a philosophical concept but as a daily experience, almost as tangible as the dogs' baying or the slow-swinging overhead draperies of the Aurora.

Suddenly—all on one day, it seems—multitudes of excited travelers arrive. The birds and animals, fish, seals, and whales: here they are! Nowhere else in the world is there a trek like the northward migration of wildlife. As soon as mild weather begins to widen the cracks in the river and sea ice, on the very morning the permafrost starts to melt on the hills, the lonely country has become crowded. The beaches, the sun-flecked waves, and the blossoming tundra, all are peopled with lives. In the sea is a shimmer of hastening fins, in the sky a network of ducks and geese, cranes, whistling swans, loons, plovers, crying out in their eagerness as they speed to their nesting sites.

For most of these creatures the North, inaccessible and remote, is the scene of their year's fulfillment. They have come for their courtships and mating; here their young will be born. They were born in the arctic themselves, and they have returned to it as their activity builds to its annual climax.

They will not stay very long, some of the male birds for less than a month. Most will be gone by the time that the first little frost-flowers form in the salty sea. But before they leave, much intense living will have occurred.

Their summer will not all be rapture. Here, as everywhere, one must fight to survive. With so many competing for partners, for homesites, and food, the issues are often dramatic.

INTRODUCTION

The fish migrating up the coast are nourishment for the white whales, which follow them. Eskimos, part of Nature's economy in the North, watch for the white whales, and killer whales sometimes attack the men; hunters become the hunted. And even the wild instincts may take the wrong turns—the lemmings, in some years, breed too fast. But surpassing the harsh, realistic happenings is the great fruition that only takes place, to this degree, in the arctic.

Why here? Of all creatures that move with the seasons, most will come north; some will journey ten thousand miles, and why is the arctic the animals' Mecca? No one knows. In some past, warmer age the center of the earth's animal population may have been here; that may be the reason why the descendants still have an urge to return. It does give them some practical benefits, such as the densely rich plankton for whales. And possibly they, like men, are pleased by the country itself.

The arctic is of course not entirely deserted in winter; it only seems so. There are living organisms on land and under the ocean's crust. With the arrival of spring many of these, too, have an impulse to push farther north. Joining the migrants from distant places, they continue until they have reached the limit of summer, the narrow strip that the seasons dispute. There the sea ice has only withdrawn from the shore for as long as the winds permit, and the permafrost in the soil will not thaw down as deep as a dozen inches. This is an icebound summer, lovely if never lush. Ice breathes its crispness into the air, while fog wraiths, born of the difference in temperature between the cold seas and the land, are blown across wide, smooth beaches. The sun shines night and day, but instead of climbing over the zenith, it circles around the horizon. Shadows are long, and the light has always the freshness and delicacy of an early morning.

On the tundra the flowers push up through their cover of lacey, pale lichens, the plants so rapidly growing that within two weeks of the day the seeds burst in the soil, the new fruits may have formed. Every living thing seems to be liberated. Now there is never a time when no bird sings, and the voices of children ring out on the beaches as often at midnight as at noon. In the lucent air the step of all creatures is light, and lightness is in their spirit. All, including men, have the happy wish to be moving about. The Eskimos, closing their winter cabins, travel in boats to camps on the seacoast and rivers, under the sky they call *seelah*, which means the entire outdoors. Some of the fish do not stay in the streams they have sought; they go back to the wider ocean. The birds are on the wing almost constantly, feeding their young, but many seem to enjoy, as well, soaring in pairs or flocks through the lambent dusk of the midnight. The walrus, the seals, the white whales, and the giant bowheads and humpbacks follow the ice floes. The caribou wander . . . as if no creature could get enough of this season, the more exquisite as it approaches eternal winter.

Sometimes, even in summer, winter takes back the surrendered ground. Sudden storms crash from the Bering Sea; on the arctic coast blizzards whirl down from the polar vastness. Snow may fall on the flowers and chill any young of the migrants left unprotected. In less perilous weather frost coats the cobwebs and etches the green plants with white.

Icebound summer—it has the tenuous beauty of things that can never be sure. Its stay is so short, scarcely with time to fade, that even as it is leaving it still seems spring.

CONTENTS

xi

KAMCHATKA

ARCTIC CIRCLE

Siberia

Cape Olyutorskiy

APPROXIMATE SOUTHERN LIMIT OF SEA ICE IN WINTER

BERING

St. Lawrence I.

Punuk Is.

BERING SEA

Cape Romanof

BOWER BANK

ALEUTIAN ISLANDS

180°

BRISTOL

REGION OF THE

Icebound Summer

where the surface of the permafrost melts
briefly and the sea ice withdraws northward

NORTH PA

skaggs

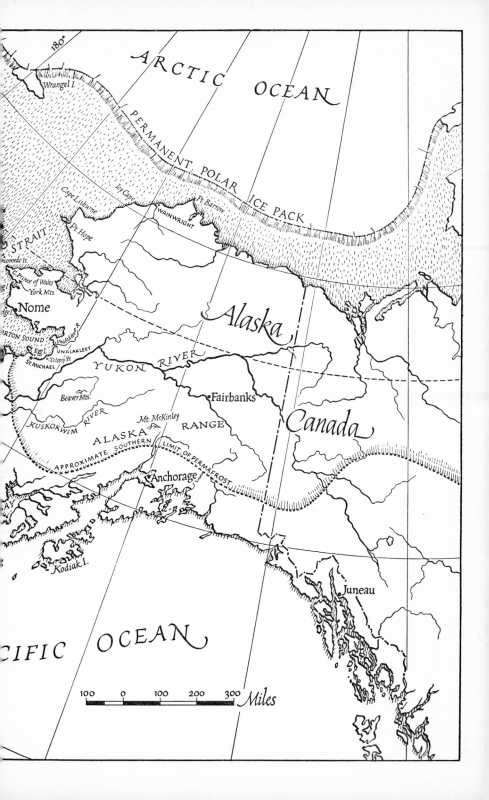

CHAPTER 1

High Tension

The lemming was very small to be bearing a
monstrous destiny. Nestled under the snow as he was, he
could have been covered by a man's hand; he could, that is,
if the hand had pressed down his long, silky, brown fur. Before going to sleep, the lemming had reached around with his
forepaws and pushed his fur up on end. Its fluff was holding
the cold away from his body, as he lay on his side with his
face buried against his hip. His jaunty little white tail was
tucked under him.

The cold was paralyzing all living flesh that it reached. A
missionary, traveling along the Yukon River not far away,
had stopped to retie his boot binding. His dog team ran after
a ptarmigan and the man, trying to hurry after them, had
found himself curiously light-headed. He was resting now in
the snow, as the lemming was, but the man would not stir
again. Nor would a snowshoe rabbit, hiding among the willows above the lemming. No intense feeling was keeping the
rabbit's energy high; and the missionary had been in the
North for so long, forty years, that his tired spirit could feel
its task finished. But the lemming would waken and instantly
would be using every means known to his tiny self to keep
warm. Apparently he was going to live until he fulfilled the
strange fate to which his needs soon would send him.

3

Other lemmings were all around him. They had been here since autumn—by now, early in March, five months in the darkness together. Their camp site was chosen well. On the edge of the Yukon trough, where the temperature was often lower than that at the North Pole, the lemmings had needed the insulation of very thick snow, and they had found it. They were up on a small plateau, a saddle between two valleys. Winds, blowing usually from the east, kept the saddle swept almost clean, but just over the western edge, where the slope started to drop away, a drift, a snow cornice several feet deep, was deposited. The lemmings were under it.

As they had foraged about, their paths had become an intricate network of snow tunnels, all of them floored at first with edible mosses and lichens. For a new meal the lemmings had only to make a new burrow. Some of the burrows led to the snow-covered boughs of willow brush, to their sweet, nourishing bark, most of it now consumed; some led to berry bushes, whose leaves, fruit, and twigs were all lemming food; and some to the remnants of winter-dried grass.

When the one lemming awoke, grass was what he craved. It was scarce but the effort to find it would be worth while. The lemming was in a state of extreme nervous tension, and just any food, such as the acid lichens, did not appeal to him. He probed out beneath the drift, clearing a passage with upward jerks of his head and forward scrapes of his feet. They were hurried, capricious movements—he went forward as if he were bumped from behind. When the search became tedious, he gave up and started to nibble the withered leaves of a buttercup plant; but he smelled a rootstock of grass and, eating along it a short way, arrived at a stalk. He snipped it off just above the runner and pulled it down through the snow.

4

Drawing it after him, he backed into himself until he became a ball, thus being able to turn around in his narrow tunnel, and ran to his nook. Months earlier he had made a nest for himself out of bits of grass, and he was snug and comfortable as he crouched there, feeding the stalk into his mouth with his forepaws. His head swayed to one side and he half-closed his eyes and chirred softly in his contentment.

All around him he heard his companions, their teeth gnawing at roots, their claws clicking along the frozen earth of denuded paths, their scamperings and bustlings, and voices—many indignant squeaks. It was a miniature hubbub, and as soon as the grass was eaten, the lemming's own voice grew higher in pitch. It became shrill whenever one of the other lemmings ran past the nest. This was the time to sleep again, but there was too much disturbance around him—and in him. He left the nest and climbed one of the burrows that led to the top of the snow. There he lay in the hole and looked out.

No grain of the snow had been stirred by the wind since he last came out, four days earlier. A few trails were showing, where other, less prudent lemmings had run about on the surface. Among these were several short spurs, disconnected trails ending lightly, just ending, giving no hint of where the lemmings that made them had gone. They were the typical tracks, hard to explain, which have caused native people in all Northern lands to call lemmings "mice from the sky." On a few other trails there was proof that some of the lemmings had ventured too far. They had been desperate to escape from their crowded confinement, frantic enough to risk a sprint in the open air . . . but their senses had suddenly blurred and their feet lost push. Soon then the snow had been cushioning small heaps of fur, as soft as the snow and quickly becoming as cold.

In normal temperatures foxes and arctic owls would have been the chief danger—they so easily saw the bright-brown lemmings wherever they ran on the snow. But those enemies had not even picked up the ones that were motionless. The predators were not coming here, either because they were trying to hide from the cold themselves, or because experience had taught them that lemmings did not often leave their burrows in weather so deadly. They could not know that the hidden colony had arrived at a state of something like mob hysteria, in which some of the lemmings were losing their fear of freezing.

The lemmings here on the saddle had been together, one generation after another, for many years. But they were not a group in the same sense as a herd of caribou or a pack of wolves that take comfort in being together. The lemmings had stayed because each of them singly found the saddle a good place to live, but they were, in fact, individualists to an extent seldom found among rodents. When they did not feel crowded, they could enjoy one another; two of them meeting would give each other a friendly nose-touch, which often became a pushing contest, a little wrestling match, just for amusement. The lemmings were sensitive, however, and excitable, and when two of them wanted the same thing, the same path, or food, or female, their tempers would flare. This year the colony was so large that the angry encounters occurred almost constantly.

The excess in their numbers was related in two ways to the weather. The preceding summer had been very warm and long for the North. Most of the females had borne four lit-

6

ters instead of two; some of the young of the year had had families, which was unusual, and a few females had even produced offspring during the winter, after some mild weeks in January. Also, and this was quite as important, the fall had been late. There had been one heavy snow, as usual, in September, but then rain. Snow and rain had alternated through all of October. The wet, soggy surface had turned into a ceiling of ice several inches thick, when the cold took its final plunge. The lemmings had kept their burrows open up through the ice as it formed, but it sealed them off from the foxes that dug them out in more normal years. In the course of an average winter many expendable lemmings were sacrificed to the foxes, a biotic arrangement that kept the colony small enough so that the rest did not intrude upon one another unbearably. Ordinarily the spring came with still no end in sight to the mat of tundra growth on which they were living. The food was not gone this year either, but some of the more savory plants, like the grass, were now hard to find. This was annoying, but chiefly the lemmings could not endure being crowded, and crowded they certainly were.

As the one that lay at the top of the burrow looked out, his westward view showed a wide expanse of low mountain peaks, a choppy land, like the sea tossed by a light brisk wind. Snow so deeply covered the summits, the slopes, and gullies that they were immaculate white except where the shadow of one lay upon another. No ridge or peak towered over the rest, but a trough curved among them, depressed as the wake of a ship will flatten a tumbling ocean. That was the Unalakleet River, solidly frozen now. When it thawed, it would flow into Norton Sound, an arm of the Bering Sea.

On the other side of the lemmings' encampment the land

dropped away to the Yukon River basin, a valley as wide as a plain. From the river, winding along the center, countless channels looped out, and off those channels others, in some places dozens more, flung farther and farther upon the plain but finally curving back into the river, with crescent-shaped islands between them.

The Yukon itself was so broad that it seemed a meandering lake. The spruces, willows, and cottonwoods that bordered its flat white surface showed from the lemming's hill as gray scratches, but over most of the plain the snow was unmarked.

Beyond the Yukon, more than a hundred miles eastward, sprawled the Beaver Mountains, shaped like beaver houses and from here looking no higher. On the far side of those was the Kuskokwim River basin and then a steep rise to the glaciers and pinnacles of the Alaska Range, and to Mt. McKinley. Scattered everywhere over the valleys were large and small lakes, meltwater on top of the frozen land in summer, and each one clearly outlined now by its paving of snow. The ponds apparently covered at least half the land. Human beings never had found a use for them, and not much use for the country around them. The scene had the uncluttered sweep of a world newly made, as clean as a cloud and bewildering in its vastness.

The snow looked white to the lemming, who could not see colors, but in fact it was tinted with mauve and gold by the sun, which was above the horizon at last, after the months of winter twilight. It was up, but too low to give any recognizable heat. The sky was empty, glittering, bone-dry, and so tautly cold that it seemed as if any small blow, a sound, the shriek of a mouse, could shatter the whole brittle dome. There

8

was no sound. No breeze rattled the leafless willows, no raven or arctic owl flapped overhead, and no airplane roared by. On days only normally cold, military planes sometimes crossed the sky on their way to Nome. One would appear at the crest of the eastern range and advance with precision over the unpeopled land; its pulsating clatter would first brush and then mangle the silence. In Anchorage now the Air Force officers looked at thermometers and, seeing them register lower than minus forty degrees, ordered the planes grounded. The lemming did not need a thermometer. When the round, plushy end of his nose started to sting, he returned to his nest.

The intense cold continued. Each day more agitated, the lemming rebuilt his nest. Running about at an erratic speed, he found a few grass stems and cut them up into inch-long pieces, and worked them into the old materials. The nest was a hollow ball with a hole at one side, loosely filling a cavity in the snow. Even after the winter's use it was still quite clean, but the lemming busied himself with making its walls more firm, with a new, fresh smell. Suddenly, though, the activity bored him. When he still had a long stem to weave into the walls, he ate it instead.

He was less and less concerned about food, however. Several times a day he would break a path into an unexplored patch of moss, or gnaw down deeply among the willow roots, but when he found what he sought, he would nibble only a mouthful or two and then would race back to his nook.

One day he was lying awake in the nest, restless, twitching his whiskers, when, with a soft rush, a female ran by. The lemming was after her instantly. He chased her as far as her own nest, and there they started to get acquainted. First they touched noses inquiringly, and the lemming sniffed over her face. The nose-touch became a push. The female ducked out around him and ran away. He followed. They came to an intersection of several burrows, where the lemming found himself fighting another male.

For a moment they only wrestled, using their forepaws but mostly weaving from side to side with a nose-grip. But the lemming resented this interruption. He shrilled at the other, a vibrating chirr, and sputtered and spat explosively. At that he expected the other to flee. When he did not, the lemming bared his teeth like a little wolf, very ferocious, a threat that was lost down here in the dark, but his imperious squeals made his meaning clear. The other, instead of leaving, attacked. The clash of the tiny tempers continued for several minutes, with the two lemmings spinning about, each trying to get his teeth in the other's throat. Finally the stranger retreated. The lemming pursued him a short way, till the loser whirled and spat out his defiance. At that he was allowed to go.

And now where could the lemming find his sweet new companion? She had vanished, but he could trail her scent. When he found her, they had a short tussle. However it came to nothing. Once more she eluded him, and the lemming suddenly felt that, anyway, he was not interested. He wanted something else, maybe a meal of lichens, maybe just a good, swift run along one of the tunnels. He went home, squealing at every lemming he met, and they all squealed back at him.

Involuntarily he was drawn into one gentle relationship during these frenzied days. Returning one afternoon to his nest, he found an infant, inquisitive like all lemmings, and therefore sniffing all over the entrance. The small one was lonely, for his mother, weakened by nursing a brood of six,

HENRY
BUGBEE
KANE

had died of the cold. He followed the older lemming into his nook and kept begging him for the friendly nose-touch. His mother had often reassured him in that way, and the lemming obliged. He did not object to having this young companion. He allowed the newcomer to move in and sleep beside him, each being warmer that way.

The cold that endangered them would break soon, in a storm as mighty as any that ever threatens the earth's inhabitants. In its earliest stages, now, the storm was only a stagnant mass of air over the Yukon valley. Into that lofty calm the permanently frozen earth was spreading more and more of its chill. With the increasing cold occurred other changes. A barometer would have shown a pressure as high above average as cyclones would show below it. Meanwhile a tension was being created between the high pressure within the center and the adjacent, normally composed air outside. For this brief time the lull was a self-contained body of atmosphere, motionless, almost as if an invisible balloon were enclosing it. But the uneven pressures could not long exist side by side.

When the lemming looked out again, there were signs of a change. It was night, and the dark sky was divided from east to west by the glowing curtain of the Aurora. It seemed to hang from the height of the stars, with its lower edge near the mountain tops, and was mostly white, with its brightness finely, vertically striped, so that its very threads showed, its threads of light. There were folds in it, and they were colored, silver-yellow, green, blue, violet, rose, like the folds in silk, whose sheen becomes iridescent where it is held in gathers.

The winds of the upper heavens were blowing the luminous fabric, so that now it swung softly, now it billowed, now it was shaken as if by a fitful breeze. As the lights and colors swept over the land, the snow was washed with the shining tints. Their reflection advanced and receded. The stars, which usually are great and brilliant in the far North, were so dimmed by the Aurora that they appeared as mere pricks in the darkness, over the gossamer sheet of light, swaying . . . majestic . . . silent.

The lemming did not pull back into his burrow at once. He was sniffing, catching a keen scent of ozone, which suggested some new kind of weather—and was the air faintly stirring?

They were very lofty winds that were moving the electrified elements of the Aurora, but they may have had an effect on the high-pressure mass just above the valley. Perhaps the fringe of the radiant gases trailed over the pool of static cold and were enough to trip the correcting forces. For the tension was breaking by morning. Spiraling out of the high-pressure area, winds were beginning to stir. Moving clockwise they were starting to circle the stagnant center. The last previous snow had been soft and thick, and the winds were picking the top of it up. Snow was rising in small swirling gusts, which soon became flurries. The winds had gained speed. The frigid and heavy air in the high-pressure mass was being spun outward, mixed with the lighter surrounding air.

Now the winds revolved at the mad pace of an escape—escape from the stress of conflicting forces. The winds were a lifeless power; yet they were tearing across the land with the same kind of wild, unchecked speed demanded by frantic nerves. Snow which had taken six days to fall was up in the air again, was a mush tautly flung ahead, more dense or more thin on the winds' waves but all blown horizontally, never given a chance to sag.

The top tiers of the racing snow were in sunshine, under a cloudless sky, with the mountain peaks standing above them, although some of the snow eddied up the slopes and was cast off the summits. The snow at ground level sped in a dusk. The drive of the winds made it needle-sharp. Three scientists, working along a creek, later told how they waited within a tent of fine-woven airplane silk, and how the snow blew through the silk and into the suitcases, closed and locked, on which they were sitting. A herd of caribou had been grazing along the foothills below the lemmings' encampment. The winds, removing the top of the snow cover, would have made it easier for them to paw through to the lichens, but few were eating. They wandered disconsolately in the mist, made miserable by the snow driving into their eyes, ears, and nostrils. A pack of five wolves, parents and young, found the storm exhilarating, however. They were thrown into the highest pitch of excitement at the chance to cut individual caribou out of the herd, with the rest not aware of what was happening and therefore not stampeding.

It was only the late snow, above the crust formed earlier, that the wind was sweeping away. The nests under the drifts were safe, although the wind penetrated the burrows. It parted the fur of the lemming and his companion, chilled their skin, and seemed to blow on their naked hearts. They were mute and motionless, apparently without life, but they only had banked their small fires during this time when the winds could have snuffed them out.

The winds were not all confined in the Yukon basin. They found their way through the breaks in the mountain barriers, passed the lemmings' divide, and swept down the Unalakleet valley. A flat tundra marsh encircled the river's mouth. The winds added its snow to their load—flung it up and away over the shelf-ice attached to the shore and extending many miles out to sea. At the farthest rim, only above the dark water there, did the winds slacken and start to let down their cargo.

Scattered over the shelf-ice were ridges, immense cakes and blocks upheaved during the winter. The gale beat against these obstructions, pushing so violently that the ice started to break at the shore. Its inner edge had remained grounded securely all winter, but now it was cracking. The present storm would not last long enough to complete the severance, but a later storm would blow all this ice out to sea.

After three days most of the loose snow had been swept off the country. The lakes and parts of the rivers were cleaned to the glare ice, and most of the shelf on the Sound was now blue and polished. The last remnants of movable snow sheeted along its surface, seeming a thin, white, ravenous fire. When the sun set beyond the ice in a golden haze, it shone back through the fleeing white snow-mist and burnished it.

Still the winds blew. But the storm's high-pressure center had started to leave, to progress down the Yukon trough toward the Bering Sea. When the center had passed out over the river's delta, it continued on south, across the Aleutian Islands. There it met the warm air approaching eastward above the Japanese Current. A new movement was set up between the warm and the cold masses, and this gyre very quickly became an augmented storm. It traveled southeast and entered the northern United States. Before it had spent itself, ships and planes were lost, houses were leveled, paths were hewn out of the forests, and many civilized people, in cities far from Alaska, felt more than a touch of fear at the unfamiliar power of the elements.

By the time the storm reached the Aleutian Islands, the tension had eased in the Yukon valley. Early the next morning the lemming stirred. He scratched himself with a quick staccato that woke his companion; then he licked and partially smoothed his fur. It was less than a thorough grooming, for he was impatient. He left the nest, and his feet spun through the drift as he tunneled upward. The orphan had caught the urgency. He was close behind.

The temperature was above zero and felt almost warm, for the snow had been glazed by the wind, and the sun, brightly reflected from it, seemed to double its heat. The sun was perceptibly higher, anyway, than it was when the storm began. Now, early in March, it was up for an hour longer each week. Within two months, by the first of May, there would be no more full darkness, even at midnight.

The lemming came to the top of his burrow and over him saw a flock of snow buntings, fluttering up from the south, tossing as waywardly as a band of white feathered butterflies. They flew rather high for sparrow-sized birds, looking haphazard and playful, as if they were only liking to be aloft in the sunny sky. Yet that wavering flight had brought them three thousand miles, from their wintering grounds on the Stateside prairies, toward an expedient goal: a nesting ground where multitudes of mosquitoes would provide plentiful food for their young. These were the males, three weeks in advance of the females, to select homesites. Of the uncounted millions of migrating birds that would nest in the North, the small buntings were first to arrive.

Now they were drifting, tumbling on, past the western edge of the saddle, seeming weightless as the overhead sun turned their wings into scraps of translucent white tissue. They would stop in many a place, wherever stands of grass lifted their seedtops above the snow, but every time they would be nearer the cove that they knew on the arctic shore. On that treeless coast, almost always in sight of the sea-ice, were nooks of the right size to fill with cups of fine grass and moss. And in each of the nests five or six downy young soon would be stretching out gaping mouths in their irresistible way: it was a happy objective.

The buntings were gone. The lemming turned his gaze over the snow and found that most of his neighbors were out ahead of him. They felt such relief to have left the confined, swarming burrows that many went leaping from place to place, rather than running. There never was anything slippery, mouselike, in their motions, for although they were only a little larger than mice, they were built differently—they were broader and chunkier. Their long fur gave them soft outlines, but they moved in abrupt ways, especially now when their nerves were like springs released.

Released—but far too many were here for the lemmings to feel any freedom. Under the snow they were closer together, but there they were not aware of the whole congregation. Now they were all in sight—lemmings everywhere. They were darting about on the surface, but no one of them had a straight run; they must dodge to avoid one another. Maddening to the single male was the sight of them—see them up in the boughs of the willows extending above the snow. They were racing upon the branches, not eating the bark or twigs, only trying to get away from their fellows. Many were fighting. The air was stung with their squeals.

The one in the burrow had a clear impulse: he would go somewhere else. He had been born on the saddle, and its food and its cover were just what he liked. Here were snowdrifts for warmth in winter and soft earth for burrowing in summer; here were the plants he wanted. But he could leave.

His burrow was near the center of the community. With a bound he left it and, turning west down the slope, sped away. The orphan was at his heels. Something new and purposeful showed in the steadiness of their gait. Their assurance attracted attention—and was contagious.

Two or three other lemmings fell in behind them; and then more. Now a small column was streaming along in their path. The column grew wider. It quickly became a magnet. By the time the leader had reached the forward boundary of the camping place, most of the colony had swung into the movement.

Their route was downhill, over snow glazed and smooth. The lemmings seemed to be freed from the limitations of muscle and bone, running so fast that their bodies swayed and the backward kicks of their feet were blurred. Wonderful was the sense of free motion—of escape from a winter-long strain. Where were they going? None cared at the start. It was enough that now they could race ahead, with nothing to block their way.

Thus did their journey begin. They were not like the buntings, migrating toward a definite destination; they were not even like the caribou on the other side of the saddle, that wandered more or less vagrantly in a search for their favorite lichens. The lemmings were not going toward anything, but away—from their own surplus numbers. Yet all, or nearly all, traveled together, so that, in seeking relief from a bane, they took their bane with them. A few remained at the camp, those that were still in their nests when the others departed. But most of them left, in an effort to find a similar but less crowded home.

CHAPTER 2

Unsentimental Mother

In the last weeks before the young hair seal was born, his mother was much alone. When she swam about under the ice pack, she stayed away from the channels below the recently frozen leads. In those lighter lanes, with thin, translucent ice above, the males would go sweeping by, several of them together. The female, with trancelike interest, was exploring beneath the thicker ice which had been frozen all winter. She was hunting for chinks in which she could make some new exit-holes. She had her own holes, several for breathing and one large enough so that she could crawl out on the top of the ice, but they were too far apart for a cub with small lungs. He would need to rise frequently for a breath, and to rest on the surface.

When the seal found a place that seemed right, she began work by breathing upon the under side of the ice. As it softened, she nibbled and clawed it out, forming a vertical tunnel. Her hind flippers held her wherever she needed to be, the webs rippling and curling, propelling her up or down. She must often stop and swim to one of her own holes for air, but finally she had completed a chimney; then two others, close together, all opening up through the ice and wide, so that a cub could climb out of the water. They froze over again each day, but the seal would bunt out the new ice with her nose and break off the pieces around the edge with her foreflippers. She kept the holes ready.

A larger task was the shelter, the "seal's igloo," the Eskimos named it, where the cub would be born and spend his first days. It was to be on the top of the ice but under a snowdrift, with its only door down to the ocean below. When she was through the ice, up within the drift, the seal scooped out her den, leaving an unbroken roof of snow. The entrance-hole was surrounded by a floor wide enough to provide a resting place for a mother and cub.

After the shelter was finished, the female seemed even more shy, more withdrawn, as she lay apart on the ice or swam through the water below it. Fewer and fewer things could attract her interest. Her emotions appeared to be like the den—cleared to receive the cub.

She had a difficult time bearing him, for his weight was nearly a fifth of hers. Her groans filled the little house. But finally, wrapped in a transparent membrane, he lay on the floor. She split open the tissue to let him breathe, and tore it off, and licked her small cub all over. His coat was wet, and she dried it by rubbing it with her foreflipper, which had its five fingers connected with webs of furred skin. The little seal's coat was not in any way like his mother's. Hers was dark-spotted gray, its hairs thin and nearly straight, while his was a long, very dense, crinkly white fuzz.

The night he was born was starry and still, and the cold over the Northern sea was as biting as acid. The cub was not nuzzling his mother for milk—not yet. He was shivering, and his cry was a heart-melting whimper. His mother lay close against him and continued to stroke his fur.

Suddenly the caress of her flipper stopped. Her breathing, all but her heartbeat, stopped. She was hearing the squeak of sled-runners on snow, and a fluttering whistle, an Eskimo imitating a ptarmigan's voice to keep his dogs sharp. The squeaks and the whistling ceased, and the snow creaked under footsteps. The seal wrapped her flipper around the cub, catching her claws in his wool, and slid nearer the exit-hole. A harpoon drove down into the den, and the sweep of an arm broke the roof. But the mother had dived with her young one.

She dared not come up in one of the new holes near the igloo. Could the cub survive the long swim to her old exit-hole? As fast as she could with her burden and her new weakness, she sped through the water beneath the ice. She knew the route well: past the rounded corners of the submerged ice caves, under a late-frozen lead, then a straight stretch below a smooth ceiling of ice. Only a little farther—but the cub was squirming convulsively, badly needing a breath. His mother could see her hole up ahead. When she reached it and lifted the cub's nose into the air he gasped and relaxed.

Even here she did not come out; she could not risk being found. She took the small seal below to the floor of the ocean, where she lay and waited, holding him with her flipper. Frequently she would rise to let him breathe. He should be out on the top of the ice having his first meal of milk, but the hunter was still too near. Apparently he would stay all night. The ice over this east end of Norton Sound was frozen into one, vast, unbroken field. The Eskimos drove their dog sleds out to the edge, to the open water, for the better chance there to find seals. Coming so far, twenty-five miles or more, they could not go back to land in one day conveniently. When they were tired, they searched for a seal's igloo in which to lie down on the reindeer skins they had brought.

On this night the seal mother cautiously reared her head several times to look over the width of the ice. The man had vanished into her partly demolished den, but the dogs were outside. Each time she came to the surface, one or more of the dogs would rise, sniffing in her direction. They were getting her scent, but they did not bark and arouse the hunter.

The cub was becoming more limp. Now his body hung slackly away from her flipper, and yet she could only wait, she could not put him up into the air and excite the dogs. Slowly the sky became pale over the distant mountains behind the shore. The sun widened above a summit. Its shine on the snow crept closer across the ice pack, throwing shadows out from each little knob and great hummock and gradually pulling the shadows back.

The next time the mother lifted her head, the man was untying the dogs from their stakes in the ice. He stepped on the runners and started the dogs, for a time guiding them in a prowling course near the igloo, doubtless hoping to find its owner. Then he turned away west, toward the water just visible on the horizon. The dogs became smaller, only the upright shape of the man could be seen, and he too disappeared behind one of the hummocks of ice cakes. The mother seal pushed her cub, unconscious now, onto the surface.

The snap in the air and the brightness revived him. For the first time alert, he started to live. But living was only a lack, a desperate want, a fumbling for—what? There it was—silky smooth cream, rich and warm, going down his throat. Pull it harder! He needed so much and probably never would get enough. The milk was filling his mouth faster than he could swallow, and yet hunger, a fearful blind dread, was not stilled. Milk was a thing that must be, and it might not be. It could stop. The seal's flippers, like small hands, curled inward, involuntarily trying to grasp, to hold.

When his stomach was full, the cub still sensed a need. He pushed forward against his mother, and cried. The sheltering body came nearer, until he was almost enclosed by it, covered and safe. A caressing tongue stroked his nose, up over his forehead, around his ears. He pushed his head closer to make the stroking more firm. His mother was rubbing his fur with her flipper, too; she was doing her wild, instinctive best to make him feel loved and soothed, and finally the cub fell asleep.

All through the day she did not leave him. If he was awake and she had stopped stroking or licking his wool he would nudge her, an eloquent asking. He did not open his eyes more than to glimpse the gray fur at his side.

Over him meanwhile spread the airy and delicate light of the North. Now at the end of winter, the sun was swinging around the horizon. Even at noon it was low, shadows were long, and the sky was spacious and lucent. On this day the sun's rays struck upward and touched a platoon of small cloud puffs, brushing gold on their under surfaces. The gold was reflected down on the ice field—on the transparent blocks of ice and on the wide, level pack, which was covered with snow except for the pale-green puddles of sea water, seeped through the tide cracks and not yet frozen. The colors would never be visible to the seal. His eyes could discover a minute fish in the shadowed water beneath the ice pack, but would not be able to show him that sunrise tints in the Northern sky make the ice glow like jewels.

On the seal's second day, when curiosity moved him to look around, he found that a pressure ridge of ice cakes towered over him. They were piled up in mammoth disorder, with jagged ice pinnacles spiking the top. The ridge, called an *eewoonuck* by the Eskimos, rose from the floor of the ice field abruptly, as mountains are sometimes thrust up from plains. But the slopes and crevices in the *eewoonuck* were not arranged as they are on a mountain, which shows the stresses that built it up and the carving of valleys by water. The ice mountain was wreckage.

The seal lay in a snow meadow close to its base. Farther away other *eewoonucks* broke the expanse, with flat snow fields around them. No sand was here, no sunken logs with root-crowns mazy and interesting, no swaying seaweed with small darting fish and lazy large ones exploring among the fronds, no shellfish speeding about by clapping their shells together. Those, in the depths below, he would learn about later. On the ice, here, no life was found; therefore no death —as if the world were just being formed, all new as yet and unspoiled, no dust, no death, only the lovely light and the clean sparkling crystal, suitable for a small, new creature, himself so white. But this realm of purity was wide, silent, and motionless. *Where was his mother?* The cub's cry was a shriek.

She was near. She splashed up at once and stretched out beside him. His sudden loneliness had been a slight shock, and so now as he nursed, the end of each breath would catch in his throat. As always, his mother was stroking his fur. Was his woolly first coat beginning to shed? By the time that his second, thinner coat had replaced it, the cub would have built up an insulating layer of fat. He then would have had all of her milk that he needed, and if she had taught him and cared for him well, she could go on to other urgent concerns. She drew her claws through his fuzz. It was tight, but it soon would loosen.

He slept, but not for long. His short period of dependence could not be leisurely. He awoke with his mother's flipper encircling him; next he was down in the water. She swam just below him, to give him a chance to cling to her back. As he felt the thrust of her muscles, the young seal had an impulse to push the same way. Safe with her support, he too curved his spine right and left and clapped the webs of his hind feet, helping to drive ahead. He was enjoying this exercise when without warning he was alone. He thrashed about, no longer able to get any grip on the water, which seemed all looseness now, broken softness. And he needed air! At the surge of his panic, his mother's strong body rose under his and they shot to the surface. But immediately he was dragged under again, and kept there until he could take a few strokes without help. Then she allowed him to go above. He caught into the edge of his exit-hole with his claws and hoisted himself—now he was back on top. He looked around anxiously. Yes, she was coming out too. He still wanted to feel protected, although he had had his first inkling of self-reliance; he had learned that a seal can swim.

She taught him to forage. As long as he kept his coat of thick fuzz he could not swim fast enough to catch fish easily, but she took him down into the water so often that soon he could find his way among the dark, glossy caverns at the submerged bases of the great *eewoonucks*. He was not startled now when flounders flapped up from the floor of the sea, like patches of mud which had drifted loose and were being wafted away. He saw king crabs fighting with slow, deadly persistence, and jellyfish throwing the living webs of their tentacles over young trout. Once a fish larger than he, a whiting, turned into an ice cave with indolent power and disappeared. But the schools of tomcod were most interesting. Spaced out evenly, they would weave through the water, feeding themselves by keeping their open mouths moving ahead. They swam at a dreamy pace, all together making their softly smooth, unhurried turns. The cub's mother flashed forward and took a tomcod in her mouth, and then worked it around until its head faced toward her throat so its fins and scales would go down comfortably. The cub did not want to eat a tomcod yet, but he did snap up a shrimp and found he could chew it.

On the top of the ice, his mother would move away over the snow while he followed. He learned how to arch his spine as she did, holding hind flippers and tail off the surface, and hitching himself along with his foreflippers, which reached ahead and gave a big push, bouncing him forward upon his belly. Always his mother would bring him back to the waterhole. He must stay near it most of the time, facing it so that one thrust with his flippers would send him below. For at this season his only enemies would approach over the ice. And finally his mother played with him. She would take the fur of his neck in her teeth and teasingly shake him. In the same spirit he snapped. She nuzzled his belly, and he rolled on his back and struck at her. She tumbled him, always so quick that when his teeth sought her skin she was out of reach. At the end she would let him catch one of her flippers. He sucked on it tensely. Perhaps with so strong a pull he could hold her forever.

All young hair seals demand their mothers' attention more than most land animals do, perhaps because they receive care for so short a time. In the seas around Norton Sound, the cubs' new gray swimming coats are grown out in two or three weeks. By that time the cubs have put on a layer of blubber that triples their weight. Needing so much milk so quickly, they plead for it almost without pause, and to make sure that they get it, nature seems to promote great affection between a seal mother and cub. The young soon learn how to make themselves very appealing, and for as long as they stay the mother seals are demonstrative. This bond was even more close in the case of the cub who was snatched from his igloo almost before he had started to breathe. His mother had had to spend more than the usual amount of time with him, for she did not have any place where she could hide him with safety, and he had become a bit spoiled. His forehead was constantly puckered, as if some uneasiness shadowed him, and when he was alone, his eyes would become huge and round, and he would stretch his head high, trying to find his guardian. Within a few days he could sit up, balancing on one hip, with a foreflipper braced on the snow, while he turned his head far around so that he had a view of the whole horizon.

If his mother was not in sight, he would begin a shrieking—desperate-sounding, and nearly always she came immediately.

But one afternoon when he called, she heaved herself out of the hole in the ice—and then wandered away. Crying, he followed. She was not playing, he sensed; she was trying to leave him. She stopped, but when he came close, she did not give him her milk at once. She kept looking off between two of the *eewoonucks*. He nudged her several times, and then finally she did turn sidewise. But why had she almost refused him?

She stirred. And the cub stopped nursing. For he could scent something new in the air. He sat up. Over his mother's side he saw, at the exit-hole, the head of another seal. It was a large head, gray like his mother's, with immense dark eyes somewhat bolder than hers. The cub's mother lifted her nose to grasp the new odor. The head of the stranger sank out of sight, rose again, and then started an up-and-down ducking. The seal mother turned her head over her back to watch, and the male's rhythmical motions continued.

A new alarm creased the cub's forehead, not fear of the male exactly, for the cub had no impulse to flee. And yet something was very wrong. He moved closer against his mother, and when she did not respond, pushed into her fur. Still he could not distract her. She swung her head forward, no longer seeming to notice the male, but she did not show the cub any affection. She brushed her cheek with her fore-flipper, and sighed, a deep, collapsing breath. Finally she began to smooth the cub's fur, behind his ears and along his chin. He felt only a little happier. He closed his eyes for a sleep but, opening them again, he saw that his mother's claws were full of white infantile wool.

HENRY
BUGBEE
KANE

In only another day or two the new situation was set: for every moment of her attention, the cub must compete with the male. His wailing rang over the ice incessantly. Sometimes, to be near her, the cub would go down in the water. She seemed to feel more responsible for him there and would keep close to him as he swam about. The male was the one who was doing the handsome swimming. Marvelous were the swift boiling somersaults, the swirling in which the big seal seemed as limber as water itself, and the speed with which he would rush past the mother and cub. That exhibition of strength would swing currents around them. In the dark water the eyeshine of the two adult seals would flash. And then, while she was watching the male, the mother might suddenly turn and play with the cub. The big seal would have to compete with *him*. It was so on the top of the ice too. The cub's mother ignored him at times, but at other times, although the male would be there and doing his best to be entertaining, she would nuzzle the little seal, play with him in the most absorbed way. It would seem then as if nothing the large seal could do would distract her. But she heard none of the cub's cries when she and the male were playing. For they did play, a grand big frolic, slapping and nudging each other and tumbling in and out of the exit-hole. It was more splendid than anything the small seal could do.

Keeping pace with the new events was the change in the cub's coat. It was now a patchwork of yellow-gray fur and tufts of an infant's white wool. The wool still impeded his swimming, while the fur made him conspicuous on the snow, so that he did not seem to belong anywhere for the present, neither down in the water nor up on the ice. A day came when his mother would never respond except when hunger put its particular tone in the cub's voice—although, at noon, she rose from the water when he had not called, and fed him, and afterwards lay on the ice beside him. She had brought up a string of seaweed, caught in her flipper. The cub sniffed it and snapped at it, pulling it off—a make-believe rival. He was having such a fine bout with it that he did not even notice his mother's leaving when she slipped down the hole.

She never came back. After his play with the seaweed he fell asleep and woke only hungry enough to whimper. But by nightfall he was quite empty, and when the sun dropped behind the *eewoonuck*, and its shadow stretched out to enclose the cub, he began to feel frightened. He sat up, turning his head to search over the silent and lifeless snow. Soon all the sunlight was gone. The stars were like frost on the sky, a sheet of sparkles that dropped its chill over the cub, while the ice breathed its cold up around him.

Perhaps his mother was over behind the *eewoonuck*. Once she and the male had gone there in their frolicking. The cub hobbled along her trail to the ridge of the ice cakes, around its end, and found the place where his mother's trail joined with the male's. But she was not there, and the ice pack seemed even emptier on this side. The cub hurried back to the water-hole. She could be there now! As eagerly as if he had heard her splash, he pulled himself forward. When he could see the hole, and no mother beside it, he still hurried. Such a need as his surely must find its answer.

All through the night the little seal cried. He demanded, he begged that his mother come. If he had not been depending on her so much, he might have found food for himself; he might have gone down in the water-hole, and that would have been more practical, for hour by hour the cold was closing the hole with ice. In the morning, when the cub dropped his nose toward the hole, it was solid. He might have broken it even then if he had tried. Instead he stayed in the air where he could make his cries heard, and by night the ice had become thick and firm. He had lost his chance to reach all the nourishing creatures down in the sea, and he had lost his escape.

Three days and nights passed. Except when he wore himself out and must sleep, he called with never a stop, so regularly that one could believe a young seal breathed like this, with a shriek every time he emptied his lungs of air. Finally he started out on a new search over the ice. Before he had gone beyond many *eewoonucks,* he heard a sound which could have been his own echo, unceasing and shrill. He went toward it, and in rounding the end of a pressure ridge found another small seal. When the other caught sight of him, he sat up and with large and astonished eyes watched him advance. The stranger had lost all of his crinkly wool; he was as smooth and sleek as an adult seal. But he too had a cub's fright and loneliness. The two sniffed each other. While they were getting acquainted at last there was silence.

The seal started back to his ice-locked hole. Would the other come? Yes, he followed. As often happens when animals move from one place to another, one proved that he was the leader. The seal retraced his trail, but when they had reached the frozen hole, no mother was there; they had nothing to do but start calling again. Now the duet of cries was impelled less by loneliness than by hunger. Neither cub had had food for several days. They were prepared for this lean time when they would begin their own foraging; because of the excess of milk they had had, they still were more fat than any young creature, even in arctic cold, needed to be. But they were very uncomfortable. Sometimes their misery would not let them rest, and they wandered about. At the foot of the ridge of ice cakes they found a hollow, enclosed by the big broken blocks. They spent more and more time there, always sleeping within its shelter.

Thus far in his life the seal had heard only the voices and splashing of his own kind, and the cracking of ice—nothing else, no sound under the whole immense sky. Even the wind had been still. But a night came when strands of cloud were drawing across the moon, and the air started to prowl. It was not yet blowing in any one direction. Swirling this way and that, faster when it spun into a nook or cranny, it seemed like a predator, whipping among the ice blocks with a low stinging hiss and turning away, an impatient and searching breath.

By morning the wind was steady. It was blowing from off the land, over the ice to the open sea. The snow previously fallen was lifted, more of it as the wind gained force, until soon the driving, blinding white mist hid everything farther away than the seal's own length. The orphans were snug in their cave, but the snow sifted in at the entrance. And the sound of the wind was a roaring confusion, a slapping and beating close to the ice, and a whistling above, as the wind went streaming over sharp slices of ice on the top of the ridge. It was a tearing, mangling wind.

Each moment felt like the storm's climax: this now was the hardest a wind could blow, this attack was its strongest. Or so it seemed; yet for two days its speed and its power increased. All sensations were one—the thundering wind, the cold, the near-darkness, and snow, all combined in a tumult.

The small seal was numb with exhaustion. He could only cling to his life, holding onto the warmth in his veins, the breath in his lungs, by a firmness that did not need to be conscious. Just hold.

The first warning of a new danger was slight—a quivering of the ice under his belly. Almost at once it was more, a crunching, a grinding, felt wherever he turned, as if some animal's teeth were gnawing the seal's own bones. He sat up, his eyes wide and alarmed. His companion also had roused. The seal hunched himself to the cave entrance. The only thing he found changed was the shine on the ice. Now the surface was gleaming and slick, all the snow blown away in the sea or shaped into fins of drift off the pressure ridges. The wind had beaten the drifts until they were glazed. Everything in the seal's view appeared brittle-hard—and the sickening vibration continued.

The wind caught the breath out of his lungs. He gasped and turned back. The other orphan had moved, trying to fit himself deeper into his corner. The seal lay down near him . . . but could not rest. He hobbled again to the entrance, and barked. He wanted the other to follow, but the small stranger did not respond, except that he opened his eyes and closed them again. He had flattened himself up against an ice block and seemed to be comforted by its solid touch. The seal too would have welcomed that reassurance, but somehow the cave was a place where one should not be. A stronger impulse was checking the seal's wish to hide.

He ventured away from the *eewoonuck*, out onto the icy, wide, sheerly unprotected expanse. The sun was setting. Breaking through layers of cloud, it was streaking the sky with brilliance, and streaking the ice below—where the slashes of light widely shifted. Swinging too was the ridge's shadow. For the pack was in motion. It had broken away from its anchorage on the shore and a flood tide had raised the ice where it was grounded along a sandbar. Floating free then, it had been propelled west by the wind's offshore pressure. The whole field of it, twenty-five miles wide, was being blown out of Norton Sound to the Bering Sea, where the large pack of arctic ice was consolidated. As the wind pushed the shore-ice along, driving upon its variously placed ridges, the vast field broke into many ice islands. Screwed by the wind and tide, these were swirling and grinding together, crashing and heaving. The seal was stunned by the colliding of tons of ice, buckling upward and falling back with a scream of slipped surfaces and a roar as of mountains crumpling.

The sunset was slow in fading. By its light the seal watched his horizon bulge and collapse. Ridges were swinging past other ridges, gaps of open water appeared and instantly closed, with always the shriek and clamor of shattering ice. The ice seemed to have its own momentum, to be some diabolical pre-historic force, unalive yet with a perverse will to destruction.

The seal suddenly felt the same panic that swept him when he had first tried to swim and he and the water went flaccid. He could no longer stay out here, alone and exposed to the violence! Hurrying back to the cave, he found the other seal in his crevice, trembling. The two curled up together, a tight huddle, sharing their warmth and their fright. But the seal could not rest. To be in the shelter was comforting—yet was not right. He went out again, moving along the foot of the ridge, and at the end, saw that the ice on the other side of the *eewoonuck* had split off from this part of the field. The open sea lay ahead. The seal's ridge, his area of the shore-ice, was now the prow of the whole wind-driven mass.

The moon, piercing through tattered clouds, showed how fast the ice was advancing into the waves. The seal went to the edge, yearning to be in the water. He dropped his nose over the brink. But the steep parapet overtook bits of seaweed and driftwood so fast that a small seal would surely be swept underneath, and suffocate there unless he happened to find a breathing-hole where the ice was not grinding.

He drew back, not to return to the nook, but to go out again on the level expanse, on the glare ice where nothing hid any part of the sky with its clouds gashed by moonlight, and nothing interrupted the sweep of the wind. To hide in the only way that he could, the seal drew his head far back into his coat with its lining of blubber. He watched his cave entrance for some sign that the other would leave the shelter and join him here on the wasteland of ice. But the shadow between the blocks showed no blur of movement. The seal's own instinct had prompted him to forsake consolation. All over the ice that night young seals were facing the same hard choice. More than half left the ridges, but some did not heed, or perhaps did not hear, the intuitive warning. Like the seal's companion, they stayed in the hideaways they had found.

They were speeding into the black water-smoke of the Bering Sea. During the winter that somber-colored mist always rose from the open leads, from water that often, itself, looked as black as tar, for the ocean floor under it was black mud. As the sea evaporated into the frigid air, reflection darkened the steam, which was whipped by the winds into tongues of black-seeming vapor, like a macabre fire. No cloud in the sky was ever as dark.

It was mid-morning when the seal on his racing ice saw through the black screen the edge of the Bering Sea ice pack. Spray from the open water had frozen upon its rim, which now had the look of a long wave, perpetually breaking. Pressure ridges lifted their shining heights from the pack, but not at the side where the Norton Sound ice was approaching. Toward that low surface the ice on which the seal rode was advancing with three days' momentum behind it.

The seal watched the foamy brink of the Bering Sea pack loom larger and clearer. It was so close now that back upon it a short way he could see a curious animal. For an instant it seemed to be an ice hummock with snow-rounded outlines, but it moved—a polar bear, lifting his head, sniffing into the wind. No doubt he was catching the scent of the seal, who raised his own head to see over the strip of black water, which was narrowing, shrinking. It was gone—

The crash knocked the seal nearly unconscious, but through his daze he could watch the frozen wave on the Bering Sea pack ride right up his pressure ridge, off its top, a great slice of ice that pushed on until it became a wide cornice that cracked off from its own weight and collapsed down the nearer slope. At the end of his old ridge a gigantic new *eewoonuck* formed, as the floors of the ice fields struck and, buckling up to a vastly high summit, tumbled back on both sides.

Debris from the mighty impact came smashing and screeching over the ice, far enough for the blocks to have struck the seal, but they did not. They stopped; the splitting and cracking spread out to remote areas of both packs. Finally the echoes of the collision had ceased. A strange animal somewhere was bellowing with pain, but otherwise all was silent.

The great slabs that had crossed the seal's ridge had demolished his shelter in falling. Where the cave had been, covered now with a block of transparent ice, lay his companion, quiet and only a little too flattened to seem alive.

The tumult went out of the seal's senses. He sat up to look around—and a movement on top of the new *eewoonuck* caught his eye. It was the polar bear, whose immense body was clambering over the ice boulders. The bear paused and srtetched out his head. His nose, far in advance of his shoulders, was weaving snake-wise as, with his poor sight, the bear tried to catch the exact direction of the seal's scent. It apparently came to him clearly, for now he was hastening down the crevices of the ridge.

Where to go! Quickly the seal must hide! Looking about, frantic, he found that near him were veins of slush, wholly demolished ice. Could he get through to the water?

He dived into the slush but did not sink. He pushed with his nose and his shoulders, squirming and driving himself below with his foreflippers. Now he stood on his head, boring down and down. A claw grazed his hind flipper, but the bear must not have realized what he touched. If the great paw scooped again into the slush, the seal did not feel it, and the vein of soft ice was not wide enough to admit the huge bulk of the bear.

After pushing down twice his own length, the seal was below the pack. He swam along under it, hardly knowing what he was seeking. But there in front of him was a great chaotic break in the ice, admitting more light—a tunnel under the pressure ridge that extended up into the air, safe, a haven.

In the long dim cavern, roofed with ice blocks, the seal climbed up onto a ledge. A black and white sea pigeon stood with its scarlet feet awash, eating a small fish, a blenny. The sight of the bird enjoying its meal reminded the seal of his hunger. He dived, straight into a school of tomcod, and caught one of them. Back in the cavern he shifted the tomcod around in his mouth and swallowed it, relishing this first taste of fish. He dived again and after a short, sharp chase captured another. The chase as well as the flavor seemed good.

Nature, the unsentimental mother, had challenged the young wistful seal. Thrown into danger he had successfully met the test, and because he had solved his own difficulties he had matured. He was no longer hungry or frightened, and he was no longer lonely, for he was not searching now for anyone who was gone.

Through a chink in the *eewoonuck* over his head, an animal's breath steamed down. It carried a scent that was new to the seal—that of an arctic fox. The fox could not reach the seal here where he lay with his foreflipper curled into water, and in any case water was safety under the ice. Water was home.

CHAPTER 3

The Foolish Fox

When the Norton Sound ice crashed into the motionless ice field outside in the Bering Sea, the impact was almost as deafening as a collision of worlds. A storm, sweeping down from the land, had cracked off the shorefast ice at the head of that great bay, the Sound. Whipping the ice westward across open water, the wind broke it up, churned it into a pandemonium of reeling ice mountains and plains, and finally hurled it into the heavier, more stable Bering Sea pack.

The seals basking upon the surface and the walrus, heavily sprawled, took the shock in their very bones. The polar bears rolled with it. But the little white foxes jumped high in the air, flying up like the shattered cakes at the edge of the floes.

After the two fields of ice came together, they remained joined by a seam of pressure ridges, long heaps of cakes and slabs where the rims buckled upward. One of the foxes started immediately to explore a ridge. With his slender black claws sharp as thorns and his soles thickly furred, he did not slip on even the glassiest slopes. He bounded up blocks of ice, jumped from one to another, wound in and out of the crevices, as sure-footed as if he had run on a ridge of rocks.

The sun put a halo around the white silk fluff of his coat, so that he looked as weightless as light itself. And so too did he act. The brink of the Bering Sea ice, where he had spent the previous weeks, had become too familiar. Now it was gone. Besides, he liked lookouts. When he did stop on the crest of the ridge, it was for the excitement of seeing the new chaotic scene below; the crystal mounds, floes, and cakes, and the frothy slush, all a dazzling confusion lit by the sun. Fresh-broken ice has a sharp, thin odor, and that too was stimulating. But soon he would whirl on again, spin around to examine some ice-encased seaweed or shrimp, and then dance ahead, a flowing line over the jagged ice, with his graceful tail giving an airy end to each movement.

He—and his nimbleness—could be discovered by anyone near enough to scent or to see a fox. He was entirely willing. Like all arctic foxes, he was so seldom in danger that he could dispense with most of the caution he would have needed if he had lived farther south. Men were the only enemies that he dreaded. On land in the winter a wolf's long legs might overtake him in deep snow; on bare ground in summer he could outrun a wolf, and he spent most of the snowy months on the ice pack, where wolves did not go. He could escape easily from the few predators that he met on that drifting and unsubstantial white plain.

His chief antagonist was a polar bear—the white bear out

there ahead, lifting his shoulders and haunches over the ridge. When the bear reached the top, he paused, and his long neck, like a giant weasel's, swung through the air to give him a scent picture of what lay below. He was a massive creature, highest over the hips, with his bulk sloping down to his shoulders and on down, now, to his nose. The weight of six men would not equal the bear's, and yet there was a sly, sinuous ease in his gait when he started over the broken ice. His motions were heavy with purpose, but so smooth that they hardly would attract more attention than if he stood still.

The wing-footed fox knew him well. For four months he had lived on the scraps from the bear's hunting. The bear did not share them willingly. He never ate all of a seal that he caught, and yet he resented the small companion who feasted on what he had left. Every time that the bear was forced to notice the fox a rumble rose in his throat. He was forever flailing out at him with his paw, and missing him, and thereafter hating him more.

The bear was stalking a cub seal, below on the Norton Sound ice. With his poor eyesight the bear had not seen the seal; his nose was leading him. But the big dark eyes of the seal kept a frantic gaze on the bear, as its little flippers slapped over the surface madly, hunching it toward a slit in the ice filled with slush. The fox was quivering with the anguish of his suspense. Now the bear must be able to see the seal. With a swinging pounce he was upon it—no, the young seal had dived. The bear scooped down with his paw, again and again, but the seal apparently had escaped. The bear ravenously wanted that tender meat. He drew back a short way and watched, alert and shrewd, doubtless expecting the seal to thrust its nose up through the slush for a breath.

The bear and the fox had not eaten for two days. And so the fox felt a personal disappointment when the bear failed to secure the seal. He wandered along the ridge, dejected. The good food was lost and besides, when emotions as fiery as his came to no fulfillment, all of his eagerness drained away. But it rose again quickly, for now he detected a small seal's odor himself, curiously up here on the crest.

The scent came from an opening between ice blocks, through which the fox could see the interior of the ridge. It was cavelike, floored with water and low, level cakes. The seal was now lying on one of them. It went into the water again, but returned with a tomcod in its mouth.

A sea pigeon too had emerged from the water and stood there below. The sharp face of the fox pressed forward. The hole was large enough so that he could jump down if he wished. Three delectable odors—a seal, a fish, and a bird! Saliva dripped from the fox's mouth. It would be a long leap however. His thick fur would protect his body in landing, but what would protect his legs, slender and delicate-boned? It

was his instinct not to risk breaking them, for those legs, trained to such speed, were his assurance of safety.

Withdrawing his head, the fox saw that the bear still was waiting beside the slush. The fox whined and pawed at the edge of the hole. The bear heard the commotion. He came up on the ridge and the fox backed along the crest. When the bear peered into the hole, he was wildly impatient to discover the seal, his seal, and not be able to reach it. He thrust one of his huge paws into the opening, tried to loosen the blocks of ice, tried with another paw, but could not dislodge them.

Now he was in a rage. And near the foot of the ridge the impudent fox was barking. The bear fairly tumbled off the ice wall and galloped after the fox. The fox led back over the rough, snow-crusted surface of the old ice pack. He stayed but a short way ahead, with the bear lunging out at him hopefully. But the bear's eyes would not permit him to catch a creature so small, white on the white snow and dodging with such agility. Finally the bear gave up. When he returned to the ridge, his motions were not smooth. He shuffled along with a loose gait, his angry eyes focused on nothing, and his head low, his nose not searching. If he could not have the fox, for the present he did not want anything else.

The fox had already forgotten him. For there, approaching over the ice, came a bird, a young glaucous gull, purely, completely white. The sky had seemed pleasing when it was domed with only the winter's exquisite soft light, but now that a bird was in it, a vast loneliness seemed to have been relieved. The gull had seen the fox. It flew over him, wheeled and dipped with a challenging cry. The fox leapt for it, missed by the length of a feather. The gull dived again. As the fox sprang, he fairly hung in the air like a frosty breath, but the gull escaped by a capriole. The fox pretended indifference. He started to sniff excitedly, as if he had found a seal's breathing-hole. The gull was not fooled. It became more and more daring. The fox joined the play again. He was not angry to be so tormented by a bird quite able to stay out of reach. When the gull circled higher, straightened its course, and left him, the fox watched it go wistfully.

Of the great flocks that soon would be coming back from the south to their arctic breeding grounds, that bird was the first that the fox had seen. Birds meant the summertime here. Even the ice pack's withdrawing and the disappearance of snow from the tundra were no greater change than the arrival of ducks, geese, loons, and others. In less than a month from this day the dense clouds of them would have settled upon the earth. Most of the birds would be mating and searching for homesites. A few weeks more and the tundra ponds would be rimmed with nests full of delicious eggs.

On the bank of one of those ponds behind Cape Prince of Wales the fox would soon join his female. It was always the same mate. They had stayed together during one winter; usually they separated, but to her he was faithful, and every spring since their first together, they had returned to each other.

They would go through the seeming uncertainty of the original courtship until, as if both had not known, again they would come together. They would spend the summer rearing their litter of cubs. After the young had scattered, the parent foxes would have a leisurely month of feasting upon the ripening berries. Where his female would go then, the fox did not know, but he always had found her back at their burrow in May.

Before long he would see her rest on the sunny sandbank. She would look beautiful to him even though her dark summer coat would be growing out through her white fur. Her eyes would be little more than slits over her vertical pupils as she, keen-sensed, would be seeing each flick of wing, and grass blade stirred by a lemming. High above, the slow-gliding longspurs, larks of the North, would sing. Together the fox and his female would be enjoying these things. She had an intensity that matched his: what other kinds of animals played their emotions on nerves strung so taut? A fox was the one with the sensitive knowing—especially that female.

For too many months the male fox had had only the company of the oppressive bear. But any day now the ice would begin to carry the fox toward his tundra burrow. On the northbound currents of spring the Bering Sea ice moved up to the strait between Cape Prince of Wales and Siberia. The strait was the portal into the Arctic Ocean; all the ice must pass through it, and there the fox always came ashore. There he would leave the bear and live on the land where he could do his own hunting.

He and the birds would arrive about the same time, and the gull may have reminded the fox. As he trotted back to the ridge, he may have been visualizing those days ahead. For when he mounted the ridge again, he threw his head up and bayed the long, songful call with the little impatient barks in it that would bring a reply from his mate if she could hear him. He called again, to the wide winter silence, unbroken except for the unceasing grumble and creak as the tide shifted the ice . . . and what? The fox heard a splash. Away toward the east the bear had dived into an open lead.

He had dropped into it with little fuss, as if he did not feel any difference between ice and water. Slowly, his white fur aflow, he paddled across the channel. Only his head was out of the surface, and was moving so quietly that it could have been a small cake of ice drifting. A fox could take pleasure in watching a polar bear's expert swimming, but when the bear climbed out on a floe the water rained back in a noisy cascade that would warn any prey.

The fox, his claws catching lightly into the ice, ran down off the ridge and across the new pack toward the bear's ice island. He too could swim, but he never did so except in emergencies. His fur was not oiled, as the bear's was, so that he always came out of the water wet to the skin and shivering. However a loose string of ice cakes led to the floe. He could jump from one to another, a feat that would call for a fox's agility and would amuse him. He did it; he reached the island dry-footed.

On this floe was a hummock, a heap of old ice cakes, and the fox found a nook near the top from which he could watch the bear. The bear had seated himself on his haunches, with forelegs straight, and was peering around the edge of a block of ice, hoping a seal would rise on the other side. His patience was endless. Noon was well past when an *oogrook*, a bearded seal almost as large as the bear, reared out of the water. Its head and shoulders shot up from the surface suddenly, buoyantly, as if the seal had been filled with air. It held itself there, vertical, while it searched for signs of an enemy. The wily bear remained motionless and the fox cooperated by refraining from even a wink.

The seal was reassured. It hurled itself out of the water onto

the ice with a powerful thrust of its back and its hind flippers
—an upward dive. Immediately it turned around so that its
foreflippers were over the edge for a quick push. Its chin
rested upon the ice. At regular intervals, equal to about fifteen
heartbeats, the seal lifted its head to make sure it was safe.
If it had been a hair seal the space of time would have been
only half as long, but the bear knew the difference. When
he began to move forward, his progress was adjusted perfectly to the seal's observations. The bear had flattened himself on the ice, legs outspread, so that he did not walk but
clawed himself forward on his fat belly. An instant before the
seal's head came up, the bear would stop. He would seem only
a white mound of snow then, and as motionless.

When the seal's coat was wet, it was dark spotted gray,
looking as much like water as any fur could. But the seal
lay in the sun until its coat had dried out to the silvery color
of ice. The bear had allowed himself all that time to approach
his victim. Now he was not more than two lengths away.
The seal's head lifted. Its hind flippers, which had been spread
to feel the sun's warmth, drew together, for the hummock's
lengthening shadow was over them. The seal stirred, its nose
tipped toward the water. The bear sprang. Hurling all his
immense weight from those prostrate legs, he was upon the
seal. With one blow of his paw, a blow seeming effortless,
he had crushed its head.

The bear's mouth moved over the carcass, absorbing the
blubber so fast that the fox could watch seal become bear
almost literally. But the seal's inner coat of firm, pliant fat
was all that the bear wanted. He stripped it off, leaving un-
touched the moist flesh beneath. The sharp little tongue of the
fox licked his lips. The bear was eating more slowly. He

rolled the seal over and was starting upon the under side when abruptly his hunger was satisfied. He shuffled, half-blind with sleep, back behind the hummock.

The fox did not wait to see him lie down, for he knew that ending. As soon as the drooping head turned away from the seal, the fox was out of his nook. He did not have the seal uncontested however. Three of the glaucous gulls had appeared from the southern sky as the bear feasted. Even while he was there, they had darted down and snatched a few bites. The bear tolerated them, but the fox would not let them near. They walked around on the ice, protesting in strident voices, or stood with their bold hazel eyes glaring resentment while they watched the food going down his throat. When the fox was so full that he too wanted to sleep he scattered the gulls with a last leap and returned to his nook. The gulls moved in for their meal. There would be gulls all the time now to share any catch made by the bear.

Although much of the big seal remained when the bear woke the next morning, he did not eat any more of it. Perhaps only warm meat appealed to him. He turned over and stretched out his short thick legs lazily. A new breeze from the warmer ocean below the Aleutian Islands was spreading a fine, light mist over the sea. The tight cold of winter had loosened. The bear dozed a while longer, at last rose to his feet. He should go back on the Bering Sea ice pack now. Why did he shamble across to the eastern side of the floe, and stand squinting out over Norton Sound?

That pack toward the east was netted with leads. On these the young ice had started to make. During the previous afternoon the channels had become encrusted with ice flowers, little pompons that formed glittering lanes as the sun caught on each crystal petal; in that lovely way did the salt water among the floes congeal in the North. By this morning, however, the small blooms had combined into a thin layer of continuous ice—"rubber-ice," as the Eskimos called it, since it bent under one's weight.

The bear let himself down off the floe. He went through the rubber-ice, but he could break a path in it easily, and he swam to the next ice pan. The fox watched from the top of the mound, where he stood tense, his eyes narrowed and ears pricked forward. The bear kept on. When he reached one of the larger floes he would climb out and amble around, hunting for signs of seal. The moving hummock would disappear from the fox's view, but beyond there would soon be a white head progressing through dark rubber-ice, the bear would hoist himself out again, or would be lost to the fox for a while. Finally he was quite gone.

The fox took a few sharp steps over the top of the mound. The bear, as well as he, should be traveling northward, for polar bears spent the summer far up on the arctic ice, the ice that never melts, the floating continent that surrounds the North Pole. If he wandered on east into Norton Sound, should the fox follow? True, the broken ice would temporarily attract seals, but the Bering Sea pack was the one that the fox knew, the one that his instinct told him he could depend on to drift toward the Strait. Alone in that ice field, how could he live? A little earlier he could have dug young seals out from under the snow, but they would all be down in the water by now. He could scrape out of the ice, and chew out, small morsels like shrimps, caught when the water where they were swimming became so cold that they did not care to move any longer. There were sure to be those; and he might, with great luck, find another bear. He would survive, though perhaps with difficulty, if he abandoned his reliable host.

The bear could be tracked by his path through the rubber-ice—if the ice would support the fox. Perhaps it was not yet thick enough. He would experiment. Spreading himself out widely, his legs flat on the ice as the bear's had been when he was stalking the seal, the fox let himself down off the edge. Very cautiously he slid forward. The ice yielded under him but it did not break until he was scrambling up the brink of another floe. Then it gave way, disintegrating rather than cracking as fresh-water ice does. Only the fox's hind legs got wet. He bounded across that floe and, exhilarated now, crept out on the new ice and eased ahead.

His progress across the ice pans was speedier than the bear's; soon the bear was in sight again, and then the fox was approaching the floe where the bear was resting. This floe carried a pressure ridge on the side. The fox circled behind it and appeared in front of the bear. He pretended that he had not seen the bear, or worse, that the bear was of no importance. As though he had found a shrimp in the ice, he gnawed at the edge of a cake. The bear may have been assuming that he had at last lost the fox. When he discovered that small exasperating figure once more in his path, he plunged for the fox so impulsively that his claw caught on a crack and he fell on his face, almost somersaulting. The fox danced around him barking. His big enemy got to his feet and took after him, scooping the air, but the fox dodged and ran up on the ridge. Their relationship was resumed. The bear still was the grudging leader, the fox the tagtail.

The rubber-ice had become too thick for the bear to swim

through comfortably, and as yet it would not hold him up. Therefore the two stayed on that floe for a brief time while the cakes, pans, and slush once more froze into a solid pack, stretching widely around them. As soon as the bear could move over it, they started to travel, seeking the edge at the open water where seals might be found again.

The smell of the water reached them the next day, and with it a new sound—in the distance a mighty mumbling. Sometimes in the summer the wind blowing back from the village of Wales had brought to the fox the voices of Eskimo men, low-pitched and heavy. The sound he heard now was like a great gathering of the men. The bear knew what it was, and he quickened his gait. Soon they came to the brink of the pack. Out in the water floated a medium-sized floe; on it was what appeared to be a black ridge. The dark mass was a herd of walrus, more than a hundred of them.

They lay close together, some even on top of others. There was unoccupied space on the floe, but it seemed that the huge creatures could not get enough of the touch and smell of their own kind, even the pressure of them, although the larger ones weighed a ton or more each. Many were murmuring and muttering, a chorus that carried over the sea with a kind of loose rhythm in it.

One of the larger bulls was sitting up, alert, often swinging his head around to survey the water. He was the sentinel. Most of the others relaxed, lying lumpishly. Against their dark hides the white tusks were gleaming, those of the males reaching well down over their chests, the females' tusks even longer. All the walrus that were not prone must keep their heads up or they would stab themselves with the tusks, and their heads rested back on their heavy necks as if the perpetual effort were tiring.

Several mothers and young were a little apart from the herd. One lay on her side, nursing her calf.

The bear slipped off into the water. He swam straight toward the walrus' floe, but most of the way he stayed under the surface. When he did come up for a breath, his white head remained motionless.

The nursing calf was through. The mother turned on her back and scratched herself with her flippers. Then she sat up, looked around, hitched herself to the edge and dived into the water. Probably she had gone down to the floor of the Sound, to dig with her tusks in its muddy bottom for clams. Her calf was asleep.

The next time the bear's head came out of the water it stayed out. But it did not move forward. It was like a dead fish that the surf brings toward a shore, pulls away, and lets drift in again. The bear seemed to be loafing. But finally it was evident that he was approaching the floe. Now his head was under the rim of ice.

Excited almost beyond endurance, the fox ran back and forth, stopped to watch, ran along again. Surely the mother walrus would soon be returning. The calf still slept, and the bear continued to wait. No—he was ready. He heaved himself over the edge and, bounding up to the calf, struck its head with his paw, killing it. He was dragging it back to the water.

The sentinel walrus discovered the bear. With a whistling bellow he roused the herd. They broke forward like an immense dark wave, all of them roaring, all plunging toward the same point—the bear with the calf. Their speed was astonishing. But the floe, large enough to support a hundred walrus, was going to capsize! The farther side rose, the surface was now a steep slope, it was vertical, the edge was an arc in the sky, and the entire walrus herd, the bear and his victim, a huge tumbled mass, were dumped in the sea. The overturned floe slapped down on the surface above them, hiding the scene while a curtain of splashing water was lifted and rained back down again.

Now all around the ice raft the water was churned with excited animals. The walrus were not alarmed because they had upset the floe; that happening was familiar to them, but they wanted that bear. Some were climbing back onto the ice, some were swimming about, all were roaring. They could allow their anger to dissipate. For the bear was dead. The sentinel walrus, his shoulders out of the water, was holding the bear in his foreflippers and drawing his tusks out of the lifeless white neck.

The fox quickly recognized his new situation: he had lost his food supply and he himself was in the wrong place, inside Norton Sound, which could become a big trap. He would go back at once onto the Bering Sea. But he soon found that he could not. When he had traveled but half a day he discovered that the Aleutian breeze had broken the Norton Sound ice away from the larger pack it had briefly joined and had driven it into its own bay again.

The fox ran along the edge of the pack until he had circled it. Just over the western horizon a strip of shine in the sky, an ice blink, meant that another ice field was lying off there. The gray sky to the south, moreover, was patched with dark bands where groves of trees interrupted the whole, sky-wide brightness which the snow-covered landscape cast up on the clouds. An Eskimo would have called that cloud picture a sky-map, and it would have told him that he was not very far from the south shore of the Sound. But the fox could not read the map, nor in any case would he swim to any objective so distant that it was out of sight.

The air became softer. An easterly wind would tear at one's fur, chew it with icicle teeth; this wind from the west merely seemed to flow over. Soon it had died completely. The tide carried the ice landward a short way and back every day; otherwise it was becalmed. It was starting to melt. The depressions on top were turning to slush, some even were puddles. A fox always should get off the ice, onto the land, when ponds of meltwater formed.

The fox's hunger was first a discomfort and then a torment. He searched along upturned slabs of ice, expecting to find shrimps, but all of his drudgery yielded him only two. Shrimps were not abundant in Norton Sound, as they were in the Bering Sea. Finally he was too tired to hunt for them. Day by day the sun dried the cover of clouds, which had spread over the sky like a layer of loose gray down. Wherever the fox ran, then, his feet kicked up bright watery splashes. But he had little impulse to run. There was no breeze to play with, and anyway, there was no tension now in his legs, which normally had as much spring as the bent switches of willow snares. And yet he was restless. Only when he became exhausted could he curl up on the ridge, with his fluffy tail over his nose, and sleep. Sometimes when he did, his feet would twitch in succession. Perhaps he dreamed that he and his female were running over the tundra. He would utter a faint bark, or small moaning cry, like a dream-form of his mating call.

One morning he woke feeling the unmistakable sway of ice being driven by waves. The wind had freshened; the pack had moved farther into the Sound and land was in view. The fox climbed the highest hummock. He sniffed in the earthy odors and narrowed his eyes to see this new country.

Behind the shore was a crescent of mountains, the points of the crescent reaching the sea in great headlands. The semi-circle of ridges, extending back from the shore and swinging toward it again, was enclosing a tundra marsh. The mountains were covered with snow, but the dark sand of the beach was bare, and the snow was gone from most parts of the marsh, except for smooth-bordered patches of white; those would be still-frozen and snow-covered ponds. A path of unbroken white emerged from the mountains and snaked through the marsh, finally reaching the sea between sandspits: a river. The land smells included some that the fox knew, grass and moss, the dank fish, salt, and seaweed odor found on all beaches, and willow brush, but he did not recognize a light pungent fragrance, that of spruces, for he never had seen a tree. He ran down to the edge of the ice and back to his perch, trembling. Land, food—and a chance to migrate back north to his mate.

This floating field on which the fox rode was the one that previously had been the shelf-ice, attached to the shore until the wind loosened it. Now the wind had returned it. Since the ice came in on a high tide, it advanced until it was grounded upon the beach. Almost as if it never had broken away, it was again a frozen rim on the east side of Norton Sound.

The fox crossed the shelf-ice, coming ashore on the south

side of the river, for on the north sandspit there was an Eskimo settlement. For the first two days he had luck. On the bank of a slough he detected the scent-mark of another fox, an odor months old but with clear meaning: buried below was a cache of food. The foxes' code regarding stored food was like that of humans—the food must not be touched unless one were desperately hungry, but a starving creature was forgiven for raiding the cache. The fox clawed off the unfrozen layer of sand, chewed and clawed when he came to the frost. He found a hoard of a dozen mice, still fresh-tasting, and ate all of them. Only a short way farther back in the marsh were runways of live mice. Standing above, he would wait till he heard a rustling and then he would leap in the air, descending with legs stiff and all four feet together. He usually had the mouse in his claws, sometimes after a scuffle. He foraged and slept alternately, and within a few days felt ready to start on his northward journey.

Or almost ready—he would delay just long enough for a little run up the river. This Unalakleet River curved sharply around a cliff, where it came out of the mountains onto the marsh, and the fox, with his enormous curiosity, had to find out what was above that bend.

He trotted along a dog-sled trail, beaten smooth on the river's frozen, flat surface, until he had reached the foot of the cliff. There he briefly turned off, tracking a hare, and found himself under willows so high that they were a ceiling above him. He never had had that experience on the barren tundra facing the Arctic Ocean. Past the cliff the river was bordered on one side by meadows and wide groves of spruces and cottonwood trees. On the other side mountains steeply rose from the river's channel, and their slopes as well were mazy with branches. His fox nature greeted this new kind of scene with delight. Here in the brush were intricate tangles where a creature could hide and watch, not being seen himself, as one always must be in his home country. Here, everywhere, were secret paths where he could vanish, he who never had had an escape except by outrunning his enemies. Thickets were over him as well as around him—as up in this cottonwood tree, its boughs quilted with snow, a black and white labyrinth. Under the dark feathery sprays of the spruces, what hideaways; among the willows what promising hunts.

On and on up the river he went, electric with his enjoyment of this adventure. In places the ice was gone, the water flowed swiftly between snow cornices, and the dog-sled trail veered to the bank. The mountains were closing in on both sides. During the breakup of previous springs the ice cakes had undercut the roots of the streamside trees. Some slanted over the channel now, and one had gone down. It spanned the river, and the fox must climb up and cross over it.

As he was making his way from the root-crown onto the trunk, he caught suddenly an amazing scent—bear! A bear, here, so far inland! The scent was not precisely like that of a polar bear, but bear it certainly was. Bear meant a meal of the food he liked best, it meant a stupid companion with which he could amuse himself, a familiar relationship. This was the climax of his good fortune.

The scent came from the other side of the river. The fox's instinct, putting together the slender tree trunk and his bear memories, reassured him about a bear's ability to come onto that unsubstantial bridge. Eager to track down the scent, the fox started over. But a strange animal, black and only a third as large as the fox's host, yet smelling like bear, was rushing out of the brush on the opposite bank. It was coming across the log, it was attacking him—

The fox tried to whirl around, lost his footing, and fell to the river below. He landed on thin ice along the edge of a torrent. As he struck, one of his forelegs broke with a sickening snap, and the ice broke, letting him down into the cold rushing water.

Sometimes under the ice, sometimes out in the open current, he was carried a long way downstream. With his injured leg he could not swim, he could do no more than get his nose out of the surface often enough for a breath. But at last he was washed by an eddy under a willow tangle. He scrambled through the wet roots and knew again the good feel of the earth.

Shaking himself dry—not easy with only three feet to grip the ground—he hobbled onto a higher level and found himself in a wide meadow bordered with spruces. The time was noon, and the sun was shining. He lay down on a munnock of grass, moss, and sprays of spicy-sweet Labrador tea. Here the warmth would finish his drying and ease the shock out of his nerves.

As he had come up the bank a flock of snow buntings, like white flower petals tossed by the wind, had fluttered aloft. They stayed over him, errantly hovering, and he could not leap for them. Such little birds, always fun in the past, would now only be tantalizing. But there, streaming across the sky, was a purple-throated loon. Its flight was as straight as the edge of the sea, and the deep swing of its wings was rapid, intense. Loons would be nesting on lakes all the way from here to the fox's own tundra. It would be easy to find their eggs. Berries, preserved by the winter's deep freeze, could be stripped from the bushes, fish in small streams could perhaps be caught. As long as the summer lasted, even a crippled fox could find food.

By fall he should reach his burrow and his mate would probably still be there. When winter came again she might stay with him, helping to capture the lemmings and mice tunneling under the snow. A fox did not have to go out on the ice with the bears; some never did. That female had been accustomed to wander about with him in the fall. Possibly she would remain with him always now, and do part of his hunting.

The eyes of the fox continued to hold on the treetop across which the loon had vanished. He might not see that particular loon again, but she was traveling in the right direction, a leader to follow, a better one than the bear. The fox licked his leg, which was aching severely. The pain would have to subside before he could travel. But he lifted his head and began to try to smell north.

CHAPTER 4

The Dark Song

The bird's northward flight was like a reversal
of time, for she had left the spring and was entering winter
again. The green landscape disappeared where the trees did,
soon after she reached the coast of the Bering Sea. Now the
landward scene was an endless brown marsh with a wide river
dividing it. The ice in the river had broken up and was tossing its way to the sea. The Eskimos thought that the moving
ice sounded like a hoarse whisper, *kusko, kusko*, and therefore had named their *kwim*, their river, the Kuskokwim. The
crunching noise reached the bird in the sky. But the speed
at which she was flying soon took her beyond it, and then
she heard only the quick *whuff, whuff, whuff* of her wings,

which had been beating for most of each day since she left
Victoria.

After she passed the Kuskokwim, the land was covered
increasingly with white snow. At the Yukon Delta the beach
showed a crust of ice, and northward the ice became wider,
stretching above the shallow sea till it met the offshore field
of loose broken floes. The bird turned out over it, for she
must keep open leads in sight, inasmuch as she was a loon
and could only alight and take off in water.

All the ice that was loose, not anchored to land, had begun
its spring drift toward the polar sea. From the loon's height
it looked smooth. Some of the ice was white; the snow had
blown off the surface of other floes, and those were of many
colors—pale green, blue, amber, and yellow, a mosaic of crys-
talline shapes fitted together and looking like marble, veined
with the sapphire water of unfrozen channels. All the colors
were visible to the bird.

The farther north she had traveled, the stronger the urge
had become to push on. All this day she had been flying, and
midnight approached. The horizontally coasting sun had slid
close to the rim of the sea. Now in May it would dip out of
sight briefly, but not long enough for true darkness to thicken.
The light never lessened much, only became more delicate,
with a shadowy shine in the air, so real that this bird flying
through it must surely, it seemed, acquire a new gloss on her
purple-black throat.

She tilted the rudder formed by the trailing webs of her
feet and began to descend. Choosing a straight lead of water
ahead, she dropped the clean arc of her body and soon was
cleaving the surface, her breast a keel and her wings held
aloft like black sails. When she came to a stop, she dived, her

slender black bill turning down on her breast with a motion that seemed to draw her below. She darted about in the liquid tunnel between the deep masses of ice, pursuing a tomcod. When she had speared it, she came up and, tossing the fish in the air, caught it head-first in her throat. She took several more and then relaxed on the surface.

Other migrating birds had come down here to rest and to forage. A few satin-black cormorants floated and splashed on the water, a single eider duck stood on the edge of the ice, his webs curling over, and a flock of emperor geese sat in a close company on a near-by floe, their slate-gray bodies as quiet as granite boulders and all their white heads facing into the southwest breeze. The loon found a mated pair of her own kind, asleep with their long necks coiled over their backs and heads under their wings.

She stayed near them, although they were not of the flock familiar to her, the several dozen Pacific loons that were her neighbors at the Alaska breeding grounds in the summer and also down at Vancouver Island during the winter. The others had made their migration without this female, but she would find them again at the nesting marsh. She had had to come north alone, for she had lingered too long, one day, on a park pond in Victoria.

During the late months of winter she had been spending her days in the park. There, under the trimmed willows and along the brushed paths, walked human beings, and those who liked birds fed the waterfowl on the little lake. The loon was wary of most of them, but in one she felt confidence. The first time she saw him, a blue overcoat was buttoned snugly around his slight, aging figure, and he was wearing a gray felt hat and suede gloves—a human being as trim as a bird. It was the courteous way that he walked, however, that made the loon feel at ease with him. For there was no aggressiveness in his gait; no secret wish to strike betrayed itself in his motions. On that sunny morning the wind was brisk. Tired after a flight against it, the loon had come down on the pond, and among other, more restless humans, discovered this man, who had met her eye and who then sat down on a bench near the water's edge and continued to watch her.

She paddled nearer to see the silver knob on his walking stick, and his hands as he folded his gloves down off his fingers, turned the gloves right-side out and laid them beside him. He took a pipe and tobacco pouch from his pocket and unhurriedly lighted a smoke for himself, meanwhile observing the bird over his hand with the match. She was propelling herself back and forth, each time nearer the line of cemented rocks at the shore of the pond.

When the man had drawn a few puffs on his pipe he took a tin box from his pocket, opened the lid, and threw a dried shrimp to the loon. Other birds, ducks and gulls, came clamoring forward, and the loon swam farther away. The man waited until the others became discouraged and left. Then he tossed a second shrimp to the loon, dropping it at the edge of the water. Inconspicuously, without any apparent movement, she let herself sink and rose with the shrimp in her gullet. It became a small plot between the loon and the man that he would feed only her, and that both of them should so manage that the rest of the birds did not notice.

The loon preferred fish to shrimps, but she found a curious pleasure in being fed by that quiet human acquaintance. She formed the habit of coming each day to the park, and he always was there. Then one morning she did not find him. The next day she returned and for several hours paddled around on the pond. In the afternoon when she went back to her flock in the harbor bay, they were gone—they had set out on their spring migration without her. Several more days the loon went to the pond, and when her friend did not appear she gathered her strength, having no other luggage, and winging up from the placid water started north on a twenty-five-hundred-mile flight alone.

Although she was young, two years old, and had made the trip north only once before, she had not lost the way. Now her journey was nearly over. Just beyond the lead where she rested the shoreline turned east into Norton Sound. That was her route; before noon she would arrive at the head of the Sound where the Unalakleet River entered it. On the surrounding marsh, spattered with ponds, soon her flock would be choosing their nesting sites. And she too would be rearing a brood—wouldn't she? This was the spring, the start of her third year, when she should find the male who would be her companion, perhaps for life. For most loons the migration was also the courting time; before they had reached the northern breeding grounds they were mated. This young female would still be single when she appeared there—but that could be true of some of the males too, surely. It was not an invariable rule that loons were paired before they had come to the end of their northward flight.

The loons' year was divided into an interlude in the alien country of docks and ships, where the sea was murky with oil, popcorn, and other refuse, and a shorter time of intense life in a wild birds' Eden. Here the sun's light came through air as pure as if no breath had ever been expelled into it. And this was the way things looked with no soot or smoke blurring them; every resting goose its precise, finely-outlined self, the brink of the ice floe showing each thread of its crystal lace, and the grass at the top of the sandy beach more than a band of vegetation—instead, a fringe of sharp, separate blades. Over everything, the blue sea, the brown and white earth, and the ice, was the nacreous tint of dawn, of the beginning, and so it would be all day.

The loon was ready to start the last lap of her journey. She turned into the Sound. Soon she had passed the rocks at Black Point, passed Tolstoy Point, where clouds of gulls were clamoring as they divided among themselves the pebbly nooks for the nests; and there at last was the swing of the shore where her river emerged between two long sandspits.

The river was frozen still, and the shelf-ice spread a few miles out over the sea—as far as the offshore bar. Many pools lay on the ice. They were silky blue-green when they were composed of sea water, an overflow through the tide-cracks, but were tea-color near the beach, where the water had drained from the land and was stained from the moss and lichens. Gulls, ducks, and geese floated around on the ponds, watching for fish, or stood on the ice digesting a meal. The fish would swim up through the cracks and out into the shallow water, where they were trapped in plain view of the birds. Arctic terns, preferring a gamier hunt, were flying along the cracks, suddenly making their sinuous downward turns as they dived. In the steamy debris on the beach, Northern phalaropes, snipes, and sandpipers ran about, catching insects as fast they hatched. And a loose flock of snow buntings tumbled aloft. They were females, the last of the spring, bound for the coastline nearest the Pole, where no vegetation was more than a few inches high, willows were vines that grew prostrate on the ground, and the cotton grass, which would reach to a man's knee at Unalakleet, on that most northern shore would but rise to his ankle.

Sandhill cranes, snow geese, and brandt were migrating over. The flocks made a web of shadow drawing across the softly glittering white expanse of the ice. Birds were everywhere. Most of those that had stopped at the marsh were known to the loon from last year, when as a juvenile she had come north, not to rear a brood, only to grow and mature. Late in the summer the birds had scattered to many parts of the hemisphere—the terns to the Antarctic, eleven thousand miles away— and now they were back at this small patch of coast, to which they had come by varying routes, but unerringly. And the loons?

Six were splashing out in the open water beyond the shelf-ice. As the female flew over, she could see tomcods milling along the lead, thousands of them, but the loons were not taking the fish. They were playing, in pairs, chasing, dipping their bills, flinging spray from their heads—three males and three females.

In the entire flock, however, were several times six. The loon turned upriver, first passing the sandspits. The channels that wound through the marsh grass were melting around the edges, and there loons were swimming, in couples. The female continued around the cliff where the river emerged from the mountains. A lake lay behind the cliff, a good nesting ground; two loons had taken possession. She followed the river farther. Many sloughs were enclosed in its elaborate turns, and on some of them she saw loons, in the inevitable pairs.

The female was hungry. She swung around to return to

the fishing grounds in the ocean. En route she passed over an arctic fox warming himself in the sun. He could be a reminder that predators would be here, foxes and wolves and the Eskimos with their guns.

Although the river appeared to be frozen, below its white, motionless surface a torrent was pouring seaward. For several weeks now the meltwater from higher creeks, entering the river, had licked out a channel within the softening ice in the stream. After this current passed out of the river's mouth, it divided and, unseen from above, flowed through some breaks in the underside of the shelf-ice. Finally cutting the sandbar, it escaped into the ocean. The loon swam along outside the sandbar until she came to the hidden flow. There she turned into the tunnels back in the ice.

A dim, blue-green light was suffused through the surface above. It showed the walls of the passageways polished smooth by the current, and it showed the harvest of last year's insects now being washed down by the melting snow on the distant mountainsides. Here many young trout were taking the insects, a feast for them. But nature, which gave generously to the fish with one hand, took away with the other hand. When the loon startled them and they swung away, their shiny sides, tilting, caught the light from above. A school of them thus became a stream of flashes, signals to any predator. Using both wings and webs, the loon overtook them easily. They were more firm and tasty than tomcods, but were not large enough to make the nourishing meal that the bird hoped to find.

She swam back to the open water beyond the ice, swung aside, and in doing so involuntarily solved her hunger problem. For the rows of white spots on her back caught the

overhead light in a way that imitated the bright streaks from
a school of small fish. A fat grayling, also foraging, shot up
out of the gloom toward the bird. The loon seized it, rose
to the surface and swallowed it. The grayling was almost too
large for her throat, but the bird worked it down, throwing
her head from side to side and arching her neck at the top to
literally pinch the fish through her gullet.

It soon became evident that the tardy female was the only
unmated loon in the Unalakleet population. She spent most
of her time off the edge of the ice, apart from the others.
Whereas they liked to float in the lee of a pressure ridge, the
female took for her own the unsheltered water farther along.
She had, of course, not started a search for a nesting site. She
spent most of her time in preening her feathers—her white
breast and black wings and her finely-striped throat—until
now she was as sleek and handsome a bird as could have been
seen anywhere on the shores of the Sound.

Before long she had one satisfaction the other loons did not
share. A young Eskimo boy began coming out to the brink
of the ice and befriending her. He had no particular wish to
kill the bird, since the taste of loon flesh did not appeal to him.
And not knowing that her natural fear of humans had broken
down, he felt flattered because she had let him approach
within reach the first time that he saw her. The next day he
had brought her one of the tomcods he had caught through
the ice for his father's dogs. Many times more he returned.
She enjoyed the chance to receive food again from a human
hand, and perhaps his companionship made her a little less
lonely.

The rest of the loons were ignoring her. They had chosen
their homesites, but making the nests was not yet their main

concern. The older birds would be using the nests of former years, and the younger ones would not start building until the ponds were completely thawed. Meanwhile they were absorbed in the yearly ritual of love.

They were high-strung birds, and one could believe that love was, for them, a very disturbing experience. During the night, in the lucent twilight, their cries spread without pause over the ice and the tundra. They were cries close to human tones, and sounding as if they expressed wild dismay. The musical cadence began with an introductory syllable, lifted to a long note, held as if waiting for an answer that never came, and then dropped to a brief, inconclusive finish. In the Eskimo village the people were kept awake—not so much by the volume of sound as by the emotion with which the cries saturated the air. The night seemed to pulse with grief, hopeless and inconsolable. Made restless, young Eskimo couples would wander out on the airstrip beyond the town, and even old women roused themselves from their reindeer-skin mattresses and went down on the sand to continue their work of gathering driftwood.

Or was the fulfillment the heartbreak? With some of the pairs of loons, now, the ritual was approaching its climax. One afternoon two of the mated birds paddled apart from the flock. For a while, with a trancelike stillness, they remained near each other. Then in perfect unison they began to swing back and forth, propelled by their webs to the left, a quick turn to the right, and back to the left. The female was low in the water, even the base of her throat was submerged, but the male was riding the ripples splendidly, with his graceful dark wings held high over his back. At the end of the dance the birds drew together, touched bills, let themselves drift apart, came near and touched bills again with an excited motion. The female of the pair suddenly dived then, in a flash of spray.

From the west a migrating loon was approaching. The spray caught his eye—or was it the single female that did? He came down in the water, a glide that furrowed the sea. When h stopped, he tilted his bill toward the sky and turned his hea side to side to survey his surroundings. He must have like what he saw, for after he caught and ate two or three fish, he idled along the edge of the ice, seeming to be in no hurry to go farther north.

His glance often fell on the unmated female. She watched him casually for a while, after which she swam back and forth with an arch in her throat and her head under the water, seeking a fish. She captured one, tossed it into the air and caught it prettily. Then she coiled her neck over her back and had a short nap. When she awoke, the new male was still there. The two of them paddled about in the water, appraising each other.

He became more daring. He began swimming past her, very near, with rapid, bold strokes. The female was agitated. She dashed away, kicking the water back with her webs, and was on the wing for a little flight over the ice.

Her young human acquaintance was there below, walking out toward the edge. Not fearing him, she did not change her course. He was carrying what seemed a bundle of strings in his hand. Actually it was a bola, a missile composed of six sinew thongs, knotted together at one end, with ivory balls attached to the other ends. The boy's father had used it in years past to snare birds, and the boy had been practicing with it.

When the loon flew above him, he whirled the balls and let go. They soared into the air and one of the thongs, touching the bird, swiftly encircled her wings. She fell to the ice, not injured but frantic to free herself. He picked her up and enclosed her body in one of his arms, with his hand firmly clasped on her throat to prevent her attacking him with her bill. When she still struggled, he gripped her head in his fingers. She fought, but he tightened his hold. Her heart was jumping. She could see nothing, but she could feel the swing of the boy's hip as he ran back to shore.

The boy took the loon into a cabin, where he wrapped a cloth tightly around her to keep her quiet, and laid her upon a table. An Eskimo woman and five or six children stood close about. They talked, in strong but relaxed voices. The small ones wanted to touch the bird, but her captor, whom the others called Isaac, kept pushing their hands away.

Isaac began to fashion a jess out of sealskin. After the jess was attached to the loon's leg, he tied the other end to a rope. Then all of the humans left, and the loon on the table could hear a hammering.

Isaac returned for her. After he fastened the rope to a stake, he removed the cloth. His family stood in a circle around the bird. Nature had placed her legs, to be most efficient in swimming, so far back that she was almost unable to walk. But she flopped and hobbled out to the end of her tether and found that it gripped and held her like some unknown enemy. Panic-stricken, she threw herself over the sand while the children laughed, all except one girl about sixteen years old. When the loon tripped, the girl untangled the rope. "Naomi! Do not let her go!" Isaac cried, darting forward. But Naomi was not releasing the bird, only trying to make her comfortable. Many

more children had gathered. Wherever she turned, all the loon could see was their brown-stockinged legs and bright calico parka-covers.

When it became quite certain that she could not escape, the loon settled upon the sand and pulled herself into her feathers. She was dazed with fear and exhaustion. Isaac brought her a dried tomcod and a pan of water, but the loon had no appetite for them. Except when she tried occasionally to flap away, she lay inert, all but unconscious.

She was not alone until evening. When she looked around then, she found that she was tied on the beach, near the last village cabin. Between her and the cabin were several dogs, each chained to a separate stake. Excited by the bird's presence, they had howled most of the day, increasing her terror. Now they had just been fed and were quiet. But dogs at the other cabins were baying. Occasionally they would all be silent, and then their clamoring sometimes started again in response to the cry of one of the loons in the water beyond the ice. The call, "Ark! Ark!" with which the loons often took flight, was picked up by the dogs. Northern huskies, the dogs themselves were unable to render a perfect bark, but the loons' voices set off their yapping.

A lane of water lay at the foot of the beach, above the ice. The loon tried to reach it, but the rope was not long enough. Her efforts attracted the children who came running to watch her. Later several adults came by. The people would stay up all night, it seemed. The sun had gone down and appeared again, and still the children were playing. But finally most of the humans were ready for sleep. Before Isaac left his new pet, he moved the fish and the pan of water in front of her.

The sun was gliding along the hilltops between north and

east. It was casting long violet shadows over the olive and wine-colored slopes, with their patches of snow, and the shelf-ice. The ponds on the ice mirrored the floating gulls and the ducks. An arctic owl foraged over the berry bushes and moss, its movements downy and hushed as it searched for lemmings. The loons' melancholy voices rose through the wide, soft, clear silence. Overhead was a dark loneliness, darkness diluted with tenuous sunlight, a distant ethereal dome pierced with stars.

Far up the beach appeared two human figures, Naomi, the Eskimo girl, and a white man taller than she. They came on at a slow pace, holding hands and sometimes in their conversation stopping to face each other. Naomi was going to show him the loon. When they drew near, she stepped ahead and took up the bird, tightly clasping her throat as Isaac had done. The man spread the toes of the loon's web with his fingers. The loon tried to draw back her bill to jab at his hand and he quickly let the foot go. Naomi put the bird back on the sand.

She and the man sat down on a driftwood log. Naomi was facing the ocean, her hands demure in her lap. Her companion straddled the log, with one foot on the top and an elbow across his knee. He took the braid that hung over the girl's shoulder and tickled her cheek with the end. Naomi's smile had a shy delight in it; her lips did not part but her eyes were unable to hide their pleasure. The man's blue eyes sent her their flash at an oblique angle.

"Ahya-keenya—with a name like that, why do you let people call you Naomi?"

"You don't like Naomi?"

"Not as well as your Eskimo name. I'll never meet any other girl with a name as pretty as Ahya-keenya."

"Missionaries gave me Naomi."

"Ahya-keenya's the name I'll always remember you by."

Naomi's face did not change by so much as a flicker; she was as still as a wild creature, freezing at danger's approach.

"You go away?" she asked, after a moment.

"As a matter of fact, I do have to leave before long," he replied. "That was something I planned to tell you."

"Where you go?"

"I'm being transferred to Kodiak. It's a bigger station—an advance for me."

"Advance?"

"A better job, I mean. I'll be making more money."

Naomi was looking out over the ice now, absently drawing her fingers along the braid. Her voice was reticent, with the least possible chance of inspiring ridicule, as she said,

"We have big house. You could live with us."

"No—no, I have to go. I'm under contract to the Government. I signed a paper promising that I'd work up here for two years, and I have to go wherever they send me."

She risked a smile again:

"After that you come back?"

"I certainly will! We'll get a boat and a tent and you and I will go fishing for a long time. That's something I've always wanted to do."

"Maybe we go now? My family have fish camp up river. Plenty wood for fires. We could trap salmon-trout all winter."

"No—that wouldn't be right. I'm surprised at you. I told you I signed a paper. Would you want me to break a promise?"

"I want you to be here. How much longer you stay?"

"I don't know—whenever they send the plane. Maybe to-morrow, maybe next week." He swung both feet to her side of the log, and taking her hand in his, touched the knuckles, one by one, with his lips.

"I'm going to miss you, Ahya-keenya." He drew her close and they were quiet except for his roving hand, to which the girl stiffened.

"You send for me?"

"You wouldn't be happy in Kodiak. Lots of big brown bears down there. Bigger than polar bears. You're afraid of bears, you know—"

With her feet nimble in their skin *mukluks* Naomi jumped up and ran toward the cabin. He ran after her, but she dodged and eluded him, entered the door and closed it. He stood outside, tapping softly a few times. Finally he tried the latch, but the door had been locked. When he came to the beach again, the loon had an instant of fright. But the man had forgotten her; his foot kicked sand over her as he passed. He picked up a rock and hurled it at one of the gulls, and then walked away up the shore toward the distant white buildings beside the airstrip.

The single migrating loon was still here at the marsh. Soon after Naomi's companion had disappeared, the bird came in over the ice, crossed the beach, and continued on toward the mountains. The male gave no sign that he was aware of the captive, but soon he returned. He flew the course several times and perhaps he did know she was there, for the last time he passed the shore his harsh cry rang out. As she watched the strong beat of his wings and then saw the spray as he landed beyond the ice, she was roused momentarily.

THE DARK SONG

After that he appeared every day. Once in the early morning when no human beings were out, he swung around and apparently paced off the strip of water between the ice and the shore. It was not long enough for a loon's landing and take off, and he returned to the open sea. He and the captive had no real relationship; yet the frequent sight of him was a tie with her own kind—enough to keep her alive. One day she accepted a fish from Isaac, and occasionally after that others, but she was growing rapidly thinner and her plumage, once so silken, had become disheveled and dusty.

Everywhere else on this coast, the urgent delights of spring were approaching their peak. Barn swallows were cutting their arcs past the cabin roof, flying in threes, one leading, two in pursuit. Even a quick eye could hardly follow their turns, the breathless straightaway and the whiplash reversal, the darting, skimming, and flinging about of the scimitar bodies that never tired. Over the edge of the beach the arctic terns, soon to break up in pairs, engaged in an aerial race that brought their gregarious months to a brilliant climax. The entire flock would mount in the sky in a wheeling cloud. At one side of their circling the gray and white feathers were almost invisible; as the curve continued, the sun flashed on the white throats and lighted a whirl of sparkles; their swing progressed, and the scraps of gold flickered out—to be kindled again when the birds came around once more.

Insistent, and closer still to the consummation, was the courtship song of the Baird sandpipers. Many times a day one of the males would rise from the tundra. His white breast, as white as if it had pressed into snow, would flash as he zigzagged upward until he had reached a certain point over a female below on the ground, where he would hover with vibrating wings a blur and his head tilting down. His vocal twirring was so long-sustained then, so commanding, and so intense that finally something must happen, the strain had to break. The little female would fly from her hiding place in the moss, and the triumphant male would come back to earth.

Pairs of longspurs were already building their nests, and the males often stopped to celebrate with aerial songs like an over-flow of contentment. One would soar into the sky as lightly as if the melody carried him up. He would glide about, high for so small a bird, letting himself down a little way, climbing again and sailing, finally descending with wings quiet, slowly drifting down of his own weight, while his joyous song spilled from his throat, liquid and sunny. The savannah sparrows had laid their eggs. One with a nest near the tethered loon sang continuously from the top of a frost mound, a heaved plat of grass. At one edge of the mound, under a tussock, his mate was sitting upon the nest, and the male bird was keeping in-truders away with the defiant earnestness of his *tsip, tsip, tseee, tseer*. There were battles too, the jaegers harassing the gulls, and the gulls competing with noisy cries, *mine, mine, mine*; but the sounds of the great festival drowned out the angry notes. From the small redpolls, the snipes, and plovers to the warbling cranes, snow geese and whistling swans pass-ing across the sky, came an outpouring of inescapable poignant voices, making the very air quiver around the loon lying so nearly dead.

One other comfort beside the attentive male was helping to keep the breath of life fluttering in her. Naomi spent many hours on the beach, and she would talk to the bird:

"Ee-lahl-looak-bis suel-lik biak-dok. Beek-thruk kleu-ickbin adow-simik."

She was saying that herring would soon arrive. They would be caught in the nets; Naomi would bring one, large and fresh, for the loon. Naomi was sewing new *mukluks* for a young sister, but the work did not progress very fast, she so often sat with her hands in her lap and eyes turned across the ice. By now it was spongy and soft—too dangerous for the dog teams to go out on it. It was breaking up into blocks with wide crevasses between, and each day was wetter and looser, each day different. But Naomi was not observing the changes. Her eyes were vacant.

Naomi was most often there in the night, when the sun only shone as a burning gold line tracing the top of the headland farther along the shore. She would stay till the first wood-chopping was heard, before breakfast. There she had solitude; there she could weep and no one observe. It was surely no help to her that the offshore loons always sang, one would say, of joys never to be fulfilled. As their dark wailing lifted and dropped away, it seemed to speak for Naomi and, as well, for the captive bird.

She had been listening to the sound one night, when her glance fell on the motionless loon. She rose to her feet and picked up the loon impulsively.

"Maybe somebody out there wait for you! You are missing somebody?" She loosened the jess from the loon's foot, and with the bird in her arms started down to the ice.

She detoured around the water along the sand and set out on the slushy surface. The most precarious ice was that where the ponds of tidewater had lain. Twice she broke through and must throw herself forward upon a browner, grainier, firmer block. She could jump across some of the cracks but had to go to the end of others; all were now mushy-bordered. In places the ice was heaved, and there it was porous; Naomi circled aside.

Finally she reached the ridge of tumbled slabs out at the edge. She walked to its end, where the ice simply disintegrated into the sea. She laid the loon on the watery surface. The loon skittered along to the sea's open depths, where she dived at once, taking her torn, dirty plumage, and her hunger, down into the haunts of fish.

Immediately she caught a trout and a few tomcods; in her present state she was not waiting for delicacies. With her hunger appeased, then, she floated and preened. She dived and splashed, dipped her head, and ran her bill down her feathers to smooth them. The food and the cold sea had already begun to revive her.

Approaching from under the water where he had seen her white breast, the single male rose at her side. With possessive and arrogant eyes he began to swim past. Each time he was nearer; now his wake washed against her throat.

Naomi had stood near the edge of the ice, watching the loon rediscover her freedom. When the male appeared Naomi smiled; when he started his courtship the smile faded, although her eyes were no less sympathetic. She turned to go. At the loon's last glimpse of her, she was making her cautious way over the ice. She was not hurrying. The beach would be lonelier now, without the bird.

On the pearly gloss of the water the male continued his sweeping march, back and forth. The movement itself was a call. The female loon felt an answering impulse beginning to stir. The next time he went by, she swung into his wake and followed him, and her motions became as one with the male bird's.

CHAPTER 5

The Sea Was Their Solace

During the arctic tests of the new, eight-engined bombers, one named the Javelin made a daily trip out from Anchorage to Nome. The Javelin flew so high and fast that the earth rolling backward beneath the wings appeared to its crew like a globe steadily turned by some unseen hand. With that view the men could observe large effects better than slower travelers. Crossing the mountain peaks west of Anchorage, they were surprised at the narrowness of so lofty a range. On the other side they could see at the same time Alaska's two mighty rivers, the Kuskokwim, flowing through forested muskeg here, and the Yukon beyond, in its more barren tundra. As the bomber came nearer to Norton Sound, again it was over mountains, but these seemed no larger than anthills. While they were covered with snow, the men had to look with care to find the Unalakleet River, which cut through, east to west, on a route paralleled by the plane.

As the snow melted off the slopes, the aviators could watch the rapid advance of the Northern spring. Yellow-brown was the first shade to come into the white, and soon the verdigris of new leaves was showing. The mountains here were beyond the limit of trees except for a few near the streams, but willow brush grew in the gullies—it appeared to the crew as pockets of faintly green smoke. Even after the snow was almost entirely gone from the slopes, the river was covered with ice:

"Glacier down there?" a new navigator inquired of the co-pilot.

"River—break up pretty soon."

"Lonely country," the navigator said, but by then the plane was out over the sea, within minutes of reaching Nome.

From cloud height the Northern landscape did appear lonely, with no road or railroad or smoke rising from human fires, with little brush where a fox could hide or a hare dart to cover, and with only those edgings of trees on the river-banks for the birds to perch in or build their nests. But the birds were living upon the ground; actually the wildlife population was dense on the tundra, and down on the frozen Unalakleet River there was a pilgrimage quite as hurried as that of the pilots. It was bound in the same direction and was spurred with a drive even more obsessed.

If the bomber crew had flown somewhat lower they might have seen the brown clot on the ice, a shade spreading back for a mile or more. It was a horde of lemmings, migrating along the valley. The small bewitched rodents were one of the earth's strangest spectacles, but the aviators were too far above to discover it.

The lemmings stayed on the river because progress was faster there. Yet the ice was rotting; its snow-covered surface was very wet. The winter trail of the Eskimos' dog sleds was on it, and water flowed in the tracks of the runners and foot-prints were puddles. The slush dragged at the little furred feet of the lemmings, but they raced forward here more easily than they could on the banks. Only the leaders needed to choose a direction. The others could follow the white tails ahead, tails which were hardly more than upturned tufts of white hair, but they clearly showed on the fur of the lemmings' rumps. The brown fur was so long that it hung down over the lemmings' hips like a wrap.

Preceding the main column of migrants were several scattered bands. The one at the head was made up of less than a dozen lemmings, and these were guided by one, a male, who was thus setting the course for the whole colony of uncounted thousands. Now he approached a stretch in the river where a swift, tumbling flow had carried away the ice. He stopped, teetering over the cornice. Would it be safe to try to swim here? Lemmings were not very powerful; shorn of their fur they would appear only slightly larger than mice. If their strength was not equal to that of the whirling stream it would spin them away, perhaps under the ice farther on, where they would drown.

The lemmings behind were crowding around the advance band. With each instant more had arrived. They were a small brown mob, milling about on the ice. The leader ended the indecision. He turned aside, off the river, up onto a sandy slope, and the rest funneled after him.

In this lower part of its course the river kept nicking in under a high bluff and looping out onto the opposite, wide, sweeping plain. Where the land was low, the swirls enclosed willow-edged marshes. The lemmings had come onto one of them. It was matted with last year's sedges, now pierced with the fresh green tips of new growth. The lemmings sped on. They arrived at a ridge of driftwood. The leader kept going. He climbed through the clutter, as agile and deft as an otter, clinging to one foothold, reaching out, gaining another, balancing, leaping, adroitly finding a way to bridge gaps —and always fast. This barrier must be passed quickly, as everything else must be done. On the other side were more of the grasslike sedges, and then a dense stand of willow brush.

At the time of its breakup the river flooded this flat. It had washed the soil out from around the roots of the willows and draped roots and branches with withered grass. The travelers worked their way through, struggling under and over. But the effort was suddenly too much. The leader fell from a bough and at first was too tired to rouse himself. When he did, he pawed out a small depression, only a vestibule of a shelter, and instantly drowned in sleep. The others also were stopped by the new demands of this thicket.

It was nearly three months since the lemmings had started their trek. In the beginning they still ate regularly, and some of them found little loving companions, and bore young. There were pauses enough so that laggards could later catch up. The farther they went however, the more urgent their pace had become. Now they were snatching their food as they ran, and not much of it, and never stopped till exhaustion had dulled their drive. On the hills at the sides of the river, ground squirrels, rabbits, and tundra voles were feasting upon the succulent leaves of spring. These were not tempting the lemmings. They ran over the tender shoots of the flat as if they knew grass only as something to step on—until their weariness was relieved. Then hunger woke them. The leader stretched out of his hole to the sod at its entrance and ate it all, even the roots. Fatigue overtook him again and, clutching a stalk of last year's crop, he fell into another sleep. Everywhere on the flat the dry seed-tops were quivering and going down, and when the lemmings' stomachs were full, once more there was quiet.

Their enemies were not resting. The lemming throng was

accompanied by another, of predators. A family of wolves had abandoned a caribou herd for this chance to gorge on the sweet flesh of lemmings, and a black bear and her yearling cubs had come part of the way, until a wolverine added his unwelcome company. When they were capturing lemmings the wolverine, out of sheer meanness, would shoulder against the bears. The mother bear knew that she might not save the cubs if he attacked. This was the season when other good foods were available, and so she had taken the cubs to less crowded pastures. Otters and minks were among the lemming pursuers. The river was home to them, but a lynx and a number of martens had come from the deeper mountains.

Several red foxes, too, made raids on the lemmings, meanwhile taking care not to become prey themselves. They stayed a little above the others. On the hillsides the soil folded horizontally as the summer-thawed surface would slip off the permafrost underneath. Creases had formed in the sliding layer and willows grew in them. The foxes were running behind these hedges. They were in very high spirits, as the poise and lift of their tails plainly showed. The wolves knew that the foxes were there. From time to time one of the wolves would climb to the top of a hill, to stand and survey the country below with his shaded eyes. When he sighted the foxes, or a ptarmigan or an arctic hare, his tail would swing, but seemingly with more anger than zest.

Finally, besides the furred hunters, the lemmings were molested by hawks and snowy owls and those slim destroying arrows, the jaegers. In their periods of abundance the lemmings always provided the great animal crop of the North, and throughout their Alaska range this spring was their peak. Next year there would appear to be no lemmings anywhere; their enemies would grow lean; many would starve. But this spring, for the predators, was a harvest.

The lemmings had come along on their migration as doggedly as if all the dangers did not exist. They could have dug under the snow, later into the soft river banks, and delayed their capture—but they could not wait. Indeed, in their normal living they had sometimes revealed themselves unnecessarily. As they bounded along their summer trails in the grass, they appeared intent on some secret plan, so pleasant it lent a sprightly eagerness to their motions. Often then they would stop in a kind of rapt pause, with their heads tilted pertly as if they were weighing delicious choices. They could be caught at those times. But now their preoccupation was different: the gaze of their eyes was fixed and filmy. And many had not bothered to make themselves shelters here at the willow flat. As they slept on top of the grass, they were curled over like infant porcupines, with their fur pushed out and their small button noses cushioned upon their chests. In a wolf's quick jaws they would not waken, they would not know any panic or pain. It was one of life's most considerate endings.

While they rested, however, quite unexpectedly they were relieved of the hovering threats. As the rays of the morning sun struck across the flat and the sedges were warmed, a few of the lemmings stirred. The leader was grooming himself. He was licking his forepaws and smoothing his face and his sides. When he finished, he turned to a female, asleep at the side of a cottongrass tussock, nudged her flank and started to sniff her face. While he was thus engrossed, a shadow appeared, moving behind the willows. The lemming froze, listening. Before he had time to dart away, one of the wolves broke out of the thicket. The lemming reared with his back to the tussock, and so furiously hissed and spat that the wolf, seeing him, actually passed him and the female by. If no other lemmings had been available, the wolf would have risked a bite on his lip, but with sleeping prey all about he could turn aside from one so belligerent.

The wolf was moving off, when he suddenly leaped in the air, fell, briefly jerked, and was still. Gun shots were snapping out from the nearest slope—all over the flat, shells were striking. Two more of the wolves were hit, and the lynx, and the wolverine.

The human hunters were Eskimos. A few weeks earlier the family had driven their dog team upriver to camp and trap squirrels for parkas. This was the time when the ground squirrels awoke from their hibernation and crept out of their burrows, still somewhat dull. Setting snares made of twine and willow bark, the Eskimos had caught enough squirrels so that they were counting this a good season when they discovered the raptorial birds circling above the flat. The men worked their way toward them, concealed by the hillside willows, and found themselves looking down on the lemming horde and the predators.

The foxes escaped in this first assault, and also some of the other quarry. The Eskimos guessed that they would come back. The men did not wish to shoot the martens and minks, and possibly ruin the valuable pelts, and therefore they worked all day making snares and setting them near the lemmings' encampment. In the dusk of the midnight the predators did return and the men captured most of them. It was a fabulous windfall. In the village out at the mouth of the river, the white trader would give the Eskimo family everything they would need for a year in exchange for the skins.

The women shot most of the owls for food, and some of the hawks and jaegers were downed by two of the smaller sons, who had their first guns and were using the birds as targets. When they came to collect the pelts, the Eskimos stood and watched the lemmings. They refrained from killing a single one, perhaps from a sense of gratitude at the great good fortune the migrants had brought.

Sleep had relaxed the lemmings. When they woke again, many besides the leader felt the old impulse to groom themselves. They were a disheveled, even a sick-seeming crowd, but they improved as they tried to make themselves clean. Although they were quick to fight at those times when their nerves were high strung, they were entirely amiable now. When two of them met they would stop for a friendly nose-push, but their tempers were not sparking. One of their typical traits was inquisitiveness. Their recent obsession to migrate, to keep moving, had silenced the questioning urges. More at ease after their rest, they could see something besides the white tails ahead.

There were strange and wonderful things in the flood wreckage lying over the flat, and the lemmings began to investigate them. One of those with the most curiosity was the leader's companion, the female. As she pawed out a tunnel under a driftwood log and came up on the other side, it seemed well to follow. Now she had found a knothole in a strip of loose bark, almost exactly the size of a burrow and fascinating to run through. The pair entertained themselves with it for several minutes. And here was an archway beneath the grass. She entered it and he with her. Beyond it the flood waters had made a pocket and filled it with pebbles. Each had a different shape and doubtless a different smell, for the pretty explorer was sniffing over each one. Of course she herself would have been fun to investigate, but she was not willing. When the male ran around in front of her and put one of his paws on her small round face, she dodged away and became absorbed, utterly, in climbing around through the roots of a spruce tree.

The tree had been torn from the riverbank by the ice of the previous spring and deposited here. Other lemmings were running upon one limb of it. They were taking turns. Always much more diversified in their actions than mice, they normally liked to devise little games, and this was one. A lemming would race to the end of the branch, jump down to the trunk of the tree, and scamper back to rejoin the others that awaited a chance on the bough. And there were other ways to enjoy oneself here. The driftwood no longer seemed like an obstruction; it was a labyrinth of intriguing nooks and connecting passageways. One could dig down through the roots of the willows too, feeling adventurous.

Much of the food at the flat had been eaten, but it was far from gone when the lemmings' liveliness became more intense. Now they were darting about in a way that seemed almost frantic. Their mood had completely changed. They were quarreling. The gentle nose-touch would always turn into a wrestling match and the lemmings would then be up on their hind legs, showing their teeth, squealing and spitting and trying to bite one another. In most cases their thick fur prevented much damage, but a few were killed. Once down, a lemming had no more interest for his opponent, however; the lemmings were not cannibals.

The roots and the driftwood had ceased to be interesting. The migrants were flying around, but now it was not to explore, it was for the activity, for the speed itself, for the release that the motion provided. The fixed look had returned to their eyes.

There were too many lemmings—that was the core of their difficulty. None wanted solitude, but a crowd of this size was a torment. Being sensitive little beasts, they became over-stimulated by superfluous numbers of their own kind. They had tried to escape, but with pitiable irony, all tried to escape together.

Back on the hillside where they had had their permanent home, the colony had increased too fast during the previous abnormally long, warm summer. Many more young had been born than in usual years and most had survived. A late fall had given alternate rain and snow a chance to form a thick icy crust over the lemming burrows, so that no predators had been able to dig them out, as would generally happen. March found a veritable swarm of lemmings trying to share a slope where perhaps a quarter as many had formerly lived, and lived in contentment and relative harmony. Their food was not gone, but the competition was now too keen for the plants they liked best, and for the females, and for the nesting sites. Their community had become too dense; wherefore life was too hectic. Month by month through the winter their tension increased until, when they came out to greet the first of the sunny spring days, an emotion like mob hysteria swept them. When one of them had an urge to leave that intolerable place, the same impulse took a few others, and then all the rest.

They had progressed at first in comparatively small bands —such numbers as were endurable to them—each of the bands seeking the easiest route of travel. There is never more than one easiest way, and since all the lemmings were quick and smart enough in their reactions to find it, they moved down the valley along the same gullies, over the same logs bridging waterfalls, across the same dunes and ponds, finally upon the flat frozen river and up on the willow marsh. They advanced on a wider front where the land was level, in a slender column wherever the path was pinched in. Their temperaments were flexible—otherwise they would not have left their familiar home; but they did not have the intelligence to realize that if any one band took the hard way, if they climbed the slope, went upstream instead of down, if they left the crowd on the river, their problem would then be solved. Before their increased numbers had made them so restless, they might even have had the initiative to take such steps—but not now. They were caught in the trap of their own fevered nerves.

The only relief they had found was movement. It could be the frenzied and senseless racing about to which they succumbed on the willow flat, or it could be a migration, a going somewhere, no one knew where but at least a straight running seemed like a search and was no doubt more satisfying than spinning around and fighting.

The same leader, again, was the one who set out, not dominating the others but giving them an example. At this far end of the marsh the river's ice was still fast to the bank. The one foremost lemming and his female companion went forward upon it. A few others joined in behind them, and then more. Now the migration had started again; the lemmings were hastening down the river.

The Javelin still made its flight over the valley each day and its crew knew something about the river that was not evident here near its mouth: the breakup had begun. Toward its headwaters the river lay in its trough like a tangled chain, and those loops and convolutions were blue. The ice had detached itself from the banks in huge cakes and blocks, and these had drifted as far as a narrow bend where the ice was still firm. They had piled up, an ice dam, and the river behind it was flooding.

On a smaller scale than above, there were jams too on the lower river. Every day some new cake, several feet thick, would come loose. The current would nudge it against the ice just below, till a second float was adrift. Soon the cakes would heap up in such a way that, for the time, they would be stationary. Behind them a pond would form. Most of the current was flowing above a layer of ice that still was attached to the river bed. However, the warmer water from off the hills was seeping along the bottom now. Often the flow on the surface would suddenly show a boiling, and out of the swirl would rise sheets of ice, bringing up sand and gravel. These would add bulk to the jams.

In their distraught state the lemmings did not avoid these masses of ice wreckage. They scrambled all through them, as if they welcomed a new demand on their energy. In the same way, too, they poured through the Eskimos' fishing camps on the banks. Every mile or so they arrived at one of the camps, which would consist of a tent frame, a rack for drying fish, and a cache, a storehouse on stilts to keep the fish away from such hungry wanderers as wolves. The structures were made of poles still encased in bark, and were easy to climb. The lemmings ran over them, up and down the supports, across the beams, into the caches—not for food, only to rid themselves of a bit of their tension.

The most soothing aid they could have was at hand, in the cool river, but its current was too torrential—the lemmings did not dare trust themselves to it. They liked water itself.

Back on their home hill they so often went into the melt-water puddles that all their summer trails seemed to seek them. Many times a lemming would crouch at rest in the spongy and saturated sphagnum, as if the cold wetness felt good to him. And now they came at last to a wide, quiet space in the river, backed up behind one of the ice dams.

The lemmings were on the bank and they could have continued along the valley by staying on land. But to swim was a short cut here. They dived in without hesitation.

They went forward in the familiar and comforting element at an astonishing speed. Their method was quite their own: half sitting up, they held their heads and shoulders well out of the surface, with their hips and hind legs much lower, entirely submerged. Their hind feet paddled furiously, propelling them, while their forefeet appeared to be used chiefly for steering.

They crossed the river as fast as they could, still seeming in haste, but when they had reached the far bank and climbed out, they shook themselves as efficiently as little dogs and then looked about with some interest. Their mood was no longer frenzied. They entered a riverside meadow, seeking its hideaways with a new ease in their motions. Obviously the water had calmed them, for they were again relaxed, of a mind to stop here and refresh themselves.

This was not like a meadow anywhere in the temperate zone. It was blanketed with a growth of plants six feet thick. The lowest layer was peat, which furnished the base for closely massed columns, tall knobs of fibers living and dead, so dense that a man's hand could hardly be thrust among them. The knobs—munnocks—were typical of the arctic. They were mushroom-shaped, separate at the bottom, with gallerylike spaces between, floored with moss. There a lemming could run about, safe from the eyes of predators. The tops of the munnocks were bushy and spread together to form a continuous surface that made the meadow look almost smooth.

The munnocks originated as cottongrass tussocks. As the new stems died every year, they became a mop of decaying plant substance, nourishment for whatever seeds fell upon them. The tussocks grew higher and higher, partly pushed up by their cores of earth, heaved into them by the frost, and partly enlarged from above. Growing out of their crowns now, besides more cottongrass, were miniature thickets composed of dwarf willows and birches, blueberry, cloudberry, and cranberry bushes, flowers like bog rosemary and arctic meadowsweet, and stalks of Hudson's Bay tea, which scented the air with its spice.

Tight as these growths were, yet there were spaces among them for rose and brown sphagnum and sprays of emerald woodland-type moss. Finally, all through and over this tangle, like an exquisite three-dimensional lace, spread lavender, white, dove-gray, and creamy-green reindeer lichens, some of them fruiting in tiny goblets with scarlet rims. This was tundra— a fairyland of the plant world, and almost every shred relished by lemmings. The multitude of the migrants arrived, they approached the meadow, and when they had reached the edge, they vanished into the munnocks' protection and bounty.

The meadow was ringed with song. Spruce and birch trees framed it, and above them Wilson snipes were weaving their loops of audible flight. Nature can make musical instruments out of unlikely materials, for the melody was produced by air passing across the birds' stiffly held outer tail feathers. It was a courtship performance. The male birds rose into the sky until they were scarcely visible, making no sound. At the top they went into a long lovely fall which, itself, caused the resonant warble. As the drop became faster, the tone became higher, and when, just over the trees, the birds made a quick upward turn, a change in the pitch was perfectly harmonized with the movement. The flight was a song as much as if human dancers, by gliding and swinging, could create music.

All this took place in the ineffable delicacy of the Northern sunlight. The sky was blue on those days, with a shimmer of green at the edge of the near-by sea. A few small stationary clouds, shaped like the finely frayed heads of the cottongrass, lay quietly just above the horizon. The air was calm. This was a world so fair that most creatures would wish they might never leave it.

The migrants' leader and his companion were spending their time in romping among the munnocks. She was not as fast on a straight run as the male, but she was quick at winding about in the lichens and berry bushes. He could catch her only by short-cutting. When he did, almost anywhere that they happened to be there was a hideaway for a tender frolic.

This was the season when the lemmings should have been making their summer burrows in newly thawed ground. That was their habit, but only a few had found any workable soil. The leader's companion was one. Less often now was she a dancer on a twig; she was vanishing into the soft earth of the river's cutbank. He followed her, although to do it he must endure having dirt kicked back into his eyes. When, however, she came to one of the wedges of clear ice which are distributed through the Northern soil, she would turn back and meet him. One fracas they had then was so fiery that it enlarged the burrow enough for a nest.

Some of the other lemmings had made halfhearted attempts to burrow, but most had found only the still-frozen fibers of peat moss. Back at their old homesite were many blisters of bare ground where the frost had churned up through the cover of plants, throwing them off to the sides. All over the North these mounds of soil were the special property of lemmings, who tunneled into their sides, into earth with its top exposed to the sun and hence warm. There were none of the frost blisters here in the meadow. It was a hospitable place to stop temporarily, but it was not the home that the migrants were seeking.

Most of the colony seemed to have only one concern, to consume as much food as they could—until a fine morning when a strong wind had arisen. It blew steadily down the valley, cold and sharp, making the air even cleaner, so that every leaf had a brilliant outline and the mountains seemed near.

The lemmings again became restless. The nourishment in the meadow would have sustained them much longer; hunger was not the cause of their discontent, but their crowded condition again had become intolerable. They did not wait for the leader's guidance. They started off, some on the ice, some on land, toward the river's mouth, which was only a few miles away. The one-time leader was so involved in his personal pleasure that he and his mate ignored their companions' departure.

Another day passed. At his home in the meadow, the lemming was keeping out of the wind. He lay in the burrow entrance, the hole in the cutbank, from which he could watch the river. His mate was at work, digging out a rear exit. The lemming crawled forward a step. His nose twitched. All the ice in the river that he could see was beginning to move. It was shifting and cracking, slowly, but with a look that seemed ominous. The whole surface, now broken, pressed forward. A rumble from up the valley was fast becoming a roar.

The female joined him, and both of them ran to the top of the bank, to a copse of small birch trees. Instinct had warned them to find an escape and the reason was soon apparent. A wall of water laden with slabs and great somersaulting cakes of ice, with whole trees, slush, willows, broken branches, and roots came tumbling down the valley. The wave in general followed the river's course but spread out past the banks. Its crashing stunned all the senses as the tumultuous mass, like a collapsing ice mountain, came sweeping forward.

The two lemmings ran up a tree trunk and, fascinated with terror, watched the first wave come even with them and pass. A flood was behind it. In these waters, also, large and small trees tossed with the ice blocks, and other trees here, especially those at the foot of the opposite, steeper riverbank, were snatched and cracked off by the force of the ice. This was the breakup, an annual crisis on all arctic rivers. The wind had been the immediate cause of it. Adding its pressure to that of the waters behind the uppermost ice dam, the wind had ruptured it. When the great wave encountered the ice fast to the lower banks, that too gave way. All at one time the river's entire shattered volume of ice came thundering down the channel.

As soon as the flood began to recede, the lemming ran to its edge and watched the swift motion. Several hours were required for the river's main burden of ice to be carried out. By the end of that time the river was back in its banks, although it still bore much wreckage, including large ice cakes.

The small homemaker was running about in the meadow, seeking a place to burrow. She could not find one, but if she would wait the riverbank would dry out. The male lemming did not share her interest. His feeling for her was ebbing. It had been like the brief, poignant arctic summer, in which from the very start there is a hint of its ending. Now in May, whenever clouds covered the sun, their shadow seemed like the darkening of a new winter; the fall of the flowers could be sensed before they had bloomed. Even if this had not been the year when the lemming's equilibrium was upset, his association with the female would have been short. Her appealing ways had delayed him, but they could not continue to hold him.

The moss at the top of the river's cutbank had broken off in the flood. He crouched there in a small gully tensely, watching the ice cakes pass. His head swung as he followed their motion, and soon he edged nearer the water. When one of the ice blocks came grinding along the bank, he jumped onto it and began to ride down the river. As the ice turned in the flow, its surface was sometimes submerged for a second or two; then his legs spun to keep him afloat. He was not quite able to equal the speed of his raft, but before he lost it, it always rose and he had its support again.

At the foot of the valley the river made one final swing to encircle the cliff that terminated the mountains. After the raft had drifted around this bend, the lemming could see a wide marsh with the river coiling across it, and two sandspits along the shore. They pointed together, forming the river's exit into the sea. All along the shore there had been a flat shelf of ice—the river's flow had gone under it. The wave of debris had broken a channel out through that shelf-ice, to the open water. The sunlit waves on the horizon were glittering among the scores of ice blocks floating upon them, the ice that the river brought down and, farther away, larger, whiter floes, remnants of sea ice.

The lemming's raft moved through the marsh, between low, level banks overhung by dense root-mats of sedges. Blue-green swallows were skimming above the banks as thickly as swarms of insects. Halfway down to the shore the raft caught on a riverbar long enough for the lemming to become agitated. He was inclined to swim to the bank, but the ice freed itself.

No trace had appeared of the other lemmings, nothing to tell whether they had entered the river after they left the meadow, perhaps to be drowned in the flood, or whether they had continued to migrate on land. As the ice cake approached the sandspits, however, the lemming could see a cloud of gulls, jaegers, and hawks hovering over the beach on the south side of the river's mouth, and over the shelf-ice beyond it. An Eskimo village covered the northern sandspit, and all the people were out on the point, looking across to the other side.

The ice raft continued its steady progress. It came to the sandspits—and when it had passed between them, the lemming discovered his old companions. The beach and the shelf-ice were brown with their numbers, a brown flood was moving across the ice toward its outer edge. Indeed it had reached the edge, and so too had the raft. The rider could recognize some of the lemmings with whom he had migrated all the way from the hillside over the Yukon valley.

Those at the head of the column arrived at the brink of the ice and plunged into the water. The others behind them also threw themselves in the waves at once. Now the brown flood was spreading over the sapphire sea, a widening flood as the ones in advance swam out farther and farther, and tens of thousands of lemmings behind them kept coming on.

The river's flow gradually was dispersed in the Sound, and the raft began moving more slowly. It was only a little faster now than the lemmings that swam beside it. The rider crept down the side and clung to the ice, close to the water's level. He saw the foam passing, the small bubbles escaped from the migrants' fur. He saw the swimmers push over the crest of the ripples and down the troughs. He saw that the white feet of some paddled more and more weakly. Their bodies then drifted flat, their heads down on the surface, although their long buoyant fur might still keep them afloat.

Out here on the sea was a motionless boat with an Eskimo boy and a white man, the village teacher, in it. They were coming home from a fishing trip and, astounded to find themselves in the midst of the migrants, had stopped the motor. The boy was standing up, watching the lemmings circle hysterically when they reached this obstruction.

"Lemmings go into the sea some place every seven years," said the boy. He was almost shouting in his excitement. "Last time my uncle, at Barrow, was out on the ice hunting walrus. Six men were camping out in a tent, fifteen miles from shore. Other men were sleeping, my uncle was the one staying awake. He was looking for walrus, but instead he saw lemmings all over the water. They climb on the ice, they go right in the tent, and my uncle always laugh when he tell how frightened those men were, to wake up and see all those kay-lung-meu-tuck."

The teacher asked him if there were as many as this time.

"For three days they go into the sea," the boy replied. "For three days they cover the beach, going into the water."

"A migration of lemmings is not like the migrations of birds and fish and some other animals," said the teacher. "Those serve a useful purpose, but these little creatures have come a long way apparently just to end their lives."

"My uncle say they are nervous. They want to keep running, that's all."

"Why does he think they swim out in the ocean, then? When they come to the shore, why don't they turn aside?"

"Maybe the water make them feel good. Maybe it take their fever away. It is so soft and cooling."

The lemmings were reaching the ice cakes. Their claws would catch into the porous sides, and they would climb up, run across, and jump in again. And now the raft came to a stop; it was only one more in the loose drift of floes that covered the sea, and the lemming left it.

Less tired than the others, he could swim faster. Indeed, many of them were still; the water was rocking numbers of small inert bodies. The larger fish and the diving birds were taking them as voraciously as the furred hunters had earlier done; yet in spite of the frigid water and the attacks of the predators, some of the lemmings were spinning ahead.

They were able to keep on going for several hours. Their old leader was one of those with the most endurance. But the size of the band still remaining grew smaller. Less than a dozen were living by night, and those, when they pulled themselves out on the frosty ice, crawled over it stiffly.

Late in the evening the sun dropped behind a low roll of clouds at the rim of the green and violet sea. Briefly its light was an incandescence along the top edge of the clouds, and then it was only a glowing magenta haze. The sky and the water had darkened. Finally the leader was quite alone—there were no other lemmings to guide. His fur, which had held the water away from his skin for a long time, was now saturated, the coldness was reaching him, even his heart felt chilled. This was a very wide river that he was trying to cross, and he was not making much progress.

Perhaps he should rest for a while.

CHAPTER 6

Luck Is Like Weather

He was only a pair of gray and white wings, passing with long, limber strokes up and down the shore— only another bird, like a slimmer gull, whose clean bit of motion was making the day seem more fresh. But stored in that head, under its cap of black feathers, were memories that human travelers would ache with envy to share. For this arctic tern, now in Alaska, had been in the antarctic two months earlier, fishing there too, but along a shore formed of ice. The ice was white above waterline, changing to emerald where it shelved away under the sea, under the Antarctic Ocean which spread its intense blue, broken sometimes by the rolling backs of whales, up to the foot of the South American continent.

During the winter the sun had shone night and day on the waves running up the green shore, and on the great, splendid birds, penguins and giant petrels, that roosted beside the terns. But finally the season of total darkness approached. The sun was leaving the south and the terns would follow it. For eight months of the year they lived in perpetual sunshine; light was their home, one could say, more than any one place was. On a morning in March, then, a signal spread through the preening flock. They poured off the ice, circled once, and straightened out toward their nesting grounds at the opposite end of the world.

No single tern acted as guide. They cooperated so well in their migrating, also in fishing, playing, nesting, and defending themselves, that they needed no dominant leader. But some were more handsome, more supple and skilled in flying and fishing than others, and one male stood out, even among the superior birds.

To excel in a flock of terns was indeed to be a fine creature. He, like the others, was silver-white on his under surfaces and pearl-gray above, with these airy colors set off by a blood-red bill and black crown. His bill, his long, narrow wings, and deeply forked tail all came to such tapering points that no eye could exactly tell where the bird ended against the sky. He seemed spirit rather than flesh and feathers, especially in action, in the flash of his dive for a fish, or perhaps the small fish had been agile himself; just over the water the tern made a sinuous, skimming recovery, was aloft, soared along with light, flexible wingbeats, but paused again, to drop lower, hover, lift into the air and then sweep away, farther out to sea.

That particular tern had strength, beauty, grace, every endowment, it seemed, except luck. Luck is like weather: it is not good or bad permanently. But during a drought it sometimes appears that the sky has lost all its windy fluency and has hardened into a brittle metallic dome; so too misfortune, a tendency to miss what he wanted, had crystallized over the life of the tern.

In the last few weeks before the flock left the south, the talented male had coursed over the ocean endlessly. He may have been only restless, but as a result of this exercise he, even more than the others, could easily maintain the cruising speed of about twenty miles an hour at which the birds traveled for eight or more hours a day. When they stopped, he would coast on the wind, pick up fish from the sea, and sleep if he could find perches of kelp. In six days he and the flock had reached the South American coast.

They continued along the Pacific side, idling there a bit, where the Humboldt Current flowed through the sea in such a way that the silt on the bottom was constantly brought to the surface. The tiny marine plants thrived on the silt, and marine animals on the plants; from the flealike amphipods to the young of barnacles, crabs, and fish, all were prospering and increasing, so that the tern could dip his bill almost anywhere in the waves and fill it. Based on the offshore islands were huge, clamoring bird communities, whose members supported themselves almost without effort because of the ocean's abundance here. But the tern was not tempted to join them. He and his fellows stayed on that sea, rimmed with the Andes' white peaks, only long enough to grow fat. The next part of the journey, past Central America, was above water so warm that few creatures could live in it. By the time that the tern had reached California however, the water was cool and food was again plentiful. For seven weeks, then, he had been on the way. Inland too, migrants, in uncounted millions, were drawing their skeins of flight northward. But the terns had come farthest, and some of their number would keep on flying until they had passed the nesting grounds of all other kinds of birds.

The tern's wings were performing this almost incredible task in order that one or two downy chicks might come into the world. This was the fourth time he had made the trip, and so far he never had had the satisfaction of putting a minnow into an eagerly pleading bill. The first year he came north, one of those scourges of terns, the jaegers, had stolen both of the eggs from him and his mate. The next year a storm at sea had delayed all the flock so that when they arrived in Alaska, it was too late for any of them to nest. On the tern's third attempt, his mate had disappeared one afternoon, a few days before the eggs had been due to hatch. Killer whales had been in the offshore water that day. Perhaps one had caught her as she was diving. The male incubated the eggs himself, but nothing came of it. Probably they were chilled some time when he left them to fish. Sixty thousand miles in the three years the tern had migrated, fruitlessly, in response to his parental hunger.

Off Peru, this spring as always, the terns were joined by a flock of the jaegers. All the rest of the way the jaegers forcibly robbed the terns of their fish, later would try to rob them of eggs and young. Other enemies on the nesting grounds might be gulls, hawks, and egg-stealing humans, but jaegers would be inevitable. Finally, the tern's own temperament could interfere with the sweet objective. A completed tern family called for so many fine points of behavior, such delicacy in his relationships, as seldom is found in the wild or the human world.

The terns' arrival, at least, was early enough this year. The male's first sight of the coast along Norton Sound showed that most of the snow was gone from the marsh and the mountains that circled it. The area where the flock nested and foraged had for its center the mouth of the Unalakleet River. The river had not broken up yet, and shelf-ice extended over the sea for about two miles. It would soon be gone; it was cracked and heaved, and half its surface was covered with blue-green ponds. Eskimos lived here beside the river, for the same reason the birds did, because it provided food. Around their cabins, built on the sandspit north of the river's mouth, was other proof that the season was right. Most of the humans were out, mending fish nets and making new boats, and children played on the beach, with a springtime lift in their voices that was not incomprehensible to the tern.

Another sandspit stretched south of the river. That beach belonged to the terns, gulls, sandpipers, phalaropes, and the basking seals. The jaegers also assumed that they had a right to space there, although their chief use for it was to stand and wait till a tern left to fish, and then follow him.

The male was so pleased to be here that during the first few days he flew about almost continuously. All of his flock did. Gradually, then, they spent more of their time on the sandspit. At first they spaced themselves evenly, but soon some of them started drawing together in pairs. Those were the mates of previous years. During the last three summers the tern himself had been one of those settled birds, but now he must find a new mate for himself, and court her.

To begin he must catch a good fish, of conspicuous size. The morning was bright and crisp when he went out to look for it. He was searching for cracks in the ice, where the water was running. There: he stopped about twenty feet over one of them. Watch below for a wisp of shadow. A marine worm was squeezing around in the water. The prongs of the tern's limber tail closed together as he prepared to dive. The worm curled out of sight and the points of the tail separated. Two Sabine gulls were in front of the tern, also fishing. The wind tipped the gulls, flung them aside, but the tern could hold himself on a line as precise as the sea's horizon, while now his wings slowly beat, wide fans of motion supporting the exquisite arc of his body. He was the quicker, more facile bird, but he was not arrogant. As he peered in the current, he kept up a musical chirping, a plaintive question: *where is that fish?*

The worm reappeared, farther behind him. The tern's head buckled down and back, with his body following through as sinuously as a snake's; then he plummeted, a sleek, vertical dive to the water. Instantly he was up, shaking the moisture out of his feathers and gulping the worm as he flew to a new hovering post.

Soon he sighted a school of small sticklebacks, filing between the blue walls of the ice. He caught two or three, hardly large enough for an offering to a female, but anyway he was hungry. A dozen more terns came skimming along the shore, and this he expected. The sociable flock always shared a good find. They poised themselves over the crack and dived in a most methodical way. The tern that discovered the fish was the one farthest left. He plunged, caught his prize and rose into the air again, taking his place at the right. As the hovering birds on the left, one by one, dived and came back on the right, gradually the original tern moved to the left and again had his chance.

The birds' voices were high and excited: *kyar, kyar,* but

they were not belligerent. This was traditional flock-fishing, and greed had no place in it. However, two jaegers had heard them. They came driving into the closely spaced, orderly flock of terns. The terns had no weapons adequate to combat the beaks of the jaegers, hooked for gouging out eyes, and their livid blue claws, webbed to make swimming easy but sharply recurved, like a hawk's, for grasping a victim. The jaegers were concentrating their siege on the tern that had made the last dive. He soon dropped the fish, and the jaeger that caught it fought for it with his fellow.

The tern flock had scattered. The single male beat his way into the wind, swung about, let it fling him back down the beach until, merely by tilting his wings and tail, he was whipped around and held motionless, now at rest on the streaming air. Before long he had seen and captured a capelin, a small fish so rich in oil that the Eskimos called it a candle-fish and, if they were not hungry, dried it and burned it for light. A capelin should tempt any female tern. With the fish dangling from his bill, he flew past the roosting grounds, slowly. He called, a pleading note: *keeer . . . keeer*. It meant, *Come*. A female soared out from the flock. She caught up with the male and, as she was passing, he gave her the fish. That was the start of a rather elaborate game. Now he was the one to follow, but he veered around quickly. She turned also and he became leader then. He allowed her to overtake him, and the fish was again exchanged. With the male in advance, the weaving chase was repeated; many times the fish was given from one to the other. In the purling grace of the fish-flight, the birds' mutual play and their timing were being tested. The timing was very important, for mated birds often engaged in swift aerial glides, duets in motion.

So far this flight was not promising. The tern saw a different female, took back his capelin, and trailed the new bird: *keeer, keeer, keeer*. She came and they flew together. She was more sensitive in her responses than the first female, more skilled at reversing quickly, exchanging the fish, and swinging away when she led. And she had a cute trick: sometimes she tossed the fish to her partner instead of passing it bill to bill. He was enjoying the flight and would have liked to continue it but the capelin was so mangled that it was going to pieces. While she was carrying it, the male came down to perch on the ice, hopefully. The female alighted too. She stood beside him and swallowed the fish. She was a young tern, not strange to the male but he never had tried a flight with her before. Now he looked at her with new interest. He was finding her nearness congenial.

The next day two startling events interrupted the romance. The first took place soon after midnight. The birds were roosting along the sandspit, with the sun, low behind them, casting their shadows down over the beach. Those of the terns were stretched out so far that they might have been sandhill cranes', but the jaegers' were longer. The actual cranes were soaring aloft, gently shaking the air with their warbling. The tern sleepily heard them and also the winnowing of the snipes. Then suddenly he was stark awake. He had detected a distant rumble, a thick, heavy crashing.

His alarm was immediately communicated to all of the terns. Like a volley of shot they were off the beach, over the ice, then the sea. The whirring and clapping of wings drowned the roaring, but as soon as the panic diminished, the new sound could be heard above the softer, light fluttering. It stirred memories of other years in some of the older birds. The male tern was one of these, and now he flew inland, with the flock following. They were above the river and found that, all the way to its mouth, the ice on the surface was breaking. The water beneath was rising, flooding the cracks. Where the marsh came to an end at the mountain slopes, the river turned out of its valley around a steep cliff. There the birds found the cause of the tumult. An immense wave of water, bearing huge ice cakes, upending trees, brush, and other debris, was pouring along the channel. The flock wheeled and followed the wave. As it spilled ahead onto the frozen river, its load was increased by the new ice it was breaking. Finally the wave smashed its way through the shelf-ice above the sea, opening out a canal to the water beyond. There the wave dispersed, and the ice, trees, sods, and floating trash lost their momentum. The tern alighted on one block of ice, flew to another, and then to a tree trunk. The flash in him was a long time in subsiding.

Late in the morning he had an impulse to fly up the now-flowing river. He started inland across the marsh, to find a spectacle far more strange than the river's breakup confronting him. Over the tundra hovered a cloud of gulls, hawks, and a multitude—hundreds, possibly thousands—of dark wings that could only be jaegers'. The birds would dart down to earth and immediately rise into the air again. The tern never had seen such a happening, and he quickened the pace of his wings.

As he drew near, he discovered a movement below in the grass. It was a flowing brown stream, not of water. He dropped lower and saw that an unbelievable number of the small rodents, lemmings, were racing along in a column. He knew lemmings; most years a few of them lived in burrows around his nest. He never had wanted to catch them, although gulls and jaegers did. But there never had been such a horde as now. And these lemmings were not seeking burrows nor trying to hide from the birds attacking them. They were progressing along toward the sea in a dense migration.

The tern soared with their predators and continued to watch as the column sped through the grass. Before many hours the lemmings had reached the sandspit and started out onto the shelf-ice. There they were altogether exposed, conspicuous dark-furred ranks, tightly packed, flinging themselves ahead in what seemed a delirium. The jaegers and gulls boiled over them, and the Eskimos watched from their side of the river.

A migration of any kind was a harvest for hunters. White men became rich catching migrating salmon; the Eskimos captured hundreds of caribou when the herds of deer poured through mountain passes; migrating fur seals were luck for the killer whales; and now the lemmings had drawn their own natural predators in a swarm that would never have congregated in any one place otherwise. From a large area of the countryside gulls, hawks, and jaegers had come as they saw neighboring birds soar away toward the Unalakleet River valley. The lemmings had followed the frozen river because it was downhill and smooth. When the river broke up, they had turned off onto the land, but they stayed near the banks. To the nesting ground of the terns they had led more of the jaegers than the male tern ever had known existed.

The lemmings had reached the sea. It was their habit to swim the small tundra ponds, and on their migration they had crossed open lengths of the river. They never had seen the ocean before, but when they looked out upon it, no doubt it only appeared to them as a wider stream. They approached the edge of the shelf-ice. Beyond were the flashing ripples.

The leaders plunged in. Swimming rapidly, they continued westward. The migrants behind jumped in after them, and then others as fast as they came. From the sea now, as well as the ice, the birds were picking them up. The ranks of the lemmings were thinning.

The tern did not stay. He had had all the excitement he wanted for one day, and moreover a sense of foreboding had filled him. He retired to the roosting grounds, but he did not preen, and he did not watch the small sandpipers and phalaropes, pecking up insects along the drift. All the tern saw was the dark cloud of wings flickering on the horizon.

The next day the jaegers still busied themselves at the edge of the ice, and the tern's depression began to lift. After a quick meal of smelts, he went on a search for a homesite. His head was filled with images of that female, and if he were going to make further progress, he had to have something more substantial to offer her than a fish.

The tern colony had their nesting grounds back on the marsh. All of the marsh was wet, since the permafrost in the ground was beginning to thaw on top, but one circular mile was a deeper basin. The Eskimos called it Grassy Lake, and that it was: a shallow lake filled with green blades already thinly tall over the surface, like green, delicate rain. The sink must once have been deeper, because a pebbly bench, an old shoreline, surrounded it. The terns' nests were along the bench, where the drop at the edge made it possible for them to enter the nests as they liked, flying in as direct as arrows.

When the male came to the lake, he found that a few pairs of terns already were making themselves at home. He flew over the plot that he and his former mate used, but he would not attempt to raise a new family there. In the terns' sensitive code of behavior, life with a second mate always began in a place with no former associations. But another homesite, one of the best, was vacant, because its owner had died in the blast of a whaler's gun during the winter. The location was up on the bench and beside a creek that flowed into the lake. From the rear the nest would be sheltered by streamside willows; sticklebacks spawned in the creek, and the young chicks could swim in it.

The tern walked about on the site, picking up twigs and leaves in his bill and throwing them over his shoulder. He scraped into the pebbly ground—here were ideal materials for a nest. His neighbors on both sides had taken possession, and the tern learned his exact boundary lines by the simple means of approaching them. When he had come too near, the other males let him know by hunching their shoulders and opening their bills menacingly. The tern spread his own bill, to show that he would defend what was going to be his, but as soon as these gestures were made, the attitude of the birds was amiable. They would even guard one another's nests on occasion, and they had established a common preening space near the nests where they would spend idle hours together. All the tern colony was divided into these smaller groups, friendly as long as the neighboring birds did not trespass.

Within a few hours that morning the tern's ownership was accepted. The custom was that he next should persuade a female to come, and present a fish to her here, this gift being a symbol. Further rituals would precede an actual mating, but today was the time for the invitation.

Something choice, something irresistible: could the tern find such an offering? Possibly an *imanyuk*? Among the small tundra ponds were a few where those savory little fish could be found. But had the fish thawed yet? Dainty and fragile-looking, black with purple above and red-spotted below, these fish did not spend the cold months in open water. They let themselves freeze as hard as the ice, in temperatures, it might be, of fifty degrees below zero. It was a dangerous practice, for when the ice cracked, some of the fish were broken in two. But most of them thawed when the ponds did, and then were as much alive as they ever had been.

As the tern sped from his homesite to one of the ponds, the breeze was a free and spacious movement under his wings. A few puffs of clouds were crossing the sky, but the sunshine was warm, reflected up from the grass as well as sent down from above. It was a day when any sweet creature should find it easy to acquiesce.

The tern hovered along the edge of a pond and found that the fins of the fish were rippling. He dived. He could have caught any number, but he did not eat even one of the fish. He flew with it to the various haunts of the tern flock and soon discovered the female. She was on the birds' bathing beach, running her bill down her feathers to sleeken them. He went over her slowly, calling. She tilted her head to watch him; he could see her do that from above. The third time he came, she rose into the air and followed.

He led straight to his nesting site, and she joined him there. When she alighted, she held her long lovely wings arched over her back for a second or two, and then suddenly folded them down. She walked through the network of shadows under the willow boughs, sensing, of course, that this was the home of the male. After a slight hesitation she came nearer. He held out the fish and she took it. But he was not pleased; she had too readily grasped it, as if they were still merely

HENRY
BUGBEE
KANE

friends, and a fish were just something to pass back and forth. He snatched it away and, lowering his head, tried to intimidate her a little. She, being so young, never had mated before, but did she not know that now he wanted her to beg prettily for his gift? He would leave her here, take the fish, make one swing around Grassy Lake, and return, and see if she might do better.

He had gone but a short way when, back from the sandspit, streaked a black dart, growing larger. No! Not at this time! Then if he must, the tern would fight. The birds came together and the jaeger attempted to beat down the tern with a blow of his wing. The tern dodged it. The jaeger was agile too, and he well knew the power in his claws and beak. But the tern's sense of outrage was almost a weapon. When the horn-colored beak would stab toward him, the tern would drive straight for one of the cold yellow eyes behind it. In and out, up and down, the birds battled—largely a vertical combat, for each tried to gain the advantage of being above. From there one could jab for the vulnerable spot at the base of the enemy's skull. It was all very fast, much quicker than human reactions, and the tern was the higher now. But the jaeger below him yanked out a beakful of down from his

thigh. The tern still held the fish. The hook on the end of the jaeger's bill struck at the side of his head, near his eye, and the startled tern let the fish go. The jaeger flew off with it.

The tern went immediately to the pond again, caught another *imanyuk*, and hurried back to his homesite. The female was gone and this time, although he searched everywhere, he could not find her.

Within a few hours the blue air was threaded with sooty-black wings, impatient wings now that the lemmings had all been consumed or drowned. Before the migrants had led the new jaegers here, there had been scarcely one parasite bird to ten of the terns. Now there were several of them for every victim. All three kinds had come, the pomarine jaegers with twisted, rudderlike tails, and also two lesser species. The smaller ones had, if possible, the more deadly spirit. No jaegers ever caught fish for themselves. Sometimes they picked up a few mice, insects, and berries, but their preference was seafood, and it was their immemorial habit to force terns and the smaller gulls, the Sabines and kittiwakes, to provide it. The terns were not large enough to defeat a persistent jaeger, and now, with the landscape so well patrolled, there was but little chance to slip off and fish for oneself unnoticed.

However, a tern could not stand on the roosting grounds, paralyzed by discouragement. The male flew to the beach of the Eskimo village, where he never had failed to find nourishment. Several jaegers trailed him. They perched on the ice near the crack, waiting. The tern could see many young trout in the current, silkenly swimming, but he would not dive. He alighted upon the sand and sat there pretending to sleep. The jaegers passed back and forth, angrily shrieking, but finally they left. Two Eskimo men walking along the shore had stopped to watch. They laughed. "Lemmings bring bad luck to the terns," one of them said.

Now the tern went to the water flowing along the crack in the ice. Only by diving could he secure a fish, but he stayed low, and with a light scalloping motion, started to pick up the craneflies on the surface. His bill would go down with a limber drop: touch, lift, dip, and touch—inconspicuous flying, yet a jaeger had seen and was speeding toward him. The tern had no fish in his bill, but he could disgorge the food in his gullet. That was what a tern often did for his hungry young, as the jaeger knew. The robber challenged him. The tern drove back at him, but except in rare circumstances a wild creature does not continue a hopeless fight. Soon the tern opened his beak and shot out the contents. The jaeger, struck in the face with it, lost it, for the food scattered over the water and ice. The tern, with a wholly disgusted *kee-kee-kee-keeear*, flew back to the sandspit.

The captivating young female was there, and he alighted beside her. She was hungry, for she also was finding it difficult to elude the jaegers. She let herself down till her breast was upon the sand, and with a soft note in her voice and a quivering of her wings, begged the male for a fish. Hunger had taught her the proper response to him, but he had nothing to offer her now. He bowed to her, lowering his head and then lifting it high. Again and again he gave her this reassurance of his regard. Still she begged. Another male edged her way. He did not have a fish either, but he wanted those winning attentions. The first male threatened the second, and the rival departed. The female appealed again to the tern.

Possibly he could find a place to fish up the river. He soared into the air. Jaegers closed in behind him, but he lost them by flying higher and higher, and circling aloft until they became discouraged. He would not descend to the main channel, above which he could see a shuttling of dark wings and light, but to a small tributary that he remembered, a haven for fingerling salmon. By a roundabout route the tern started to spiral down. But there is no secrecy in the sky, no concealment. He was a long way above the streamside trees when the unmistakable sooty forms began gathering in the air below.

If he could not catch a fish, a few other foods were acceptable for himself—berries and insects. They never had been anything but accessories in his diet; now however, he would attempt little by little to make a meal of them. A low ridge crossed the marsh, higher ground that supported crowberry bushes. From the wing he was snatching a few of the berries, but jaegers were on the ridge, picking the berries too. It would not do to let them suspect that he was accumulating a gulletful, and so the tern went to the borders of Grassy Lake. Evening approached and mosquitoes were plentiful. He caught some of them, and as soon as his hunger was party appeased, the thought of the female grew strong in his mind. He found her flying along the sandspit.

Together they went to the bathing beach, which was the sandy end of a narrow lake just behind the seashore. A dozen or more of their flock hovered over the water. Even now, in their troubled state, they bathed with a strict regard for their tern decorum. Only one, bird-sized space in the water was suitable for a bath, so it seemed. As in their flock-fishing, a single tern at a time dropped down to the surface. The male and his young companion joined the others idling on the wing, waiting. When they were next, the female alighted on the acceptable place, dipped her head, and fluttered a spray. Rising, shaking the water out of her feathers, she flew to the sand, where she bowed to the birds already assembled there, grooming themselves. The male followed the same routine and joined her. Now again she came to him, begging. His foraging had been slow, and the first berries that he had picked were by now digested. But the later ones and the insects were still in his throat. With a purpose that she at once recognized, he put his bill into her mouth and pumped out the food, as he would for a nestling chick.

Soon the two flocks, of terns and of jaegers, had worked out a program which allowed both to subsist. From the terns it required so much effort on so little nourishment, that they probably would not keep it up very long. For the present however, the days went like this:

Halfway between midnight and noon, at what would have been dawn if the sun had not shone through the night, the terns would start out to fish. They knew that they would be robbed, but a gnawing stomach will outwit logic. The robbers took all of the terns' catch for an hour or more—sometimes so many fish that a jaeger would be unable to rise on the wing until part of the food had digested. After that early period the terns, really wearied, went back to their roost, and the jaegers flew off to the tundra. When the terns started to fish again, they were allowed to keep some of their prey. A similar routine took place twelve hours later.

The jaegers were faring so well that most of them had begun to nest. The terns had not. Some were deserting their homesites, and none had laid any eggs. In only a few more days the season would be too late, but they had no heart, and many had not strength enough, for the great fruition. Moreover they needed some of the fish they caught for the amenities of their mated life. The male knew from experience how he and the female would have spent alternate times on the nest, how one seldom would have returned to relieve the other without bringing a token. The absent one would have come winging in, calling, and at the precise instant of the sweeping arrival, the other bird would have taken the fish and would be aloft. The dear ways: the companionship felt between the bird incubating and the one preening or roosting near; the bowing whenever one of them walked toward the other; and above all, the aerial glide, an assertion of love that would not have ceased when the young were grown—would they ever know these? Such fulfillment could only occur if the material needs of their lives were not too demanding. The male tern still fed his friend when he could, and they even had one or two quickly interrupted fish-flights. The relationship still was tender, but as the days passed it was sensed more dimly.

Instead of the image of nestlings, there had begun to stir in the male's mind the memories of the antarctic ice, of the distant green shore. But meanwhile the ice on this Northern coast was giving a little aid to the terns. The ice off Alaska's shores is always an unpredictable element in the lives of fish, seals, and whales, of waterfowl, and of men. "Ice never the same," as the Eskimos say, because, from the time the ocean begins to freeze, in September, until it is clear again, in July, the strong arctic winds shift the ice about, drive it away and back, tumble it, pile it on other ice and on beaches. The ice seldom is gray; itself blue, green, brown, white, or snow-covered, it reflects the sea's color, and the sun paints it with fire. The ice always is beautiful, and it may be helpful—or greatly menacing.

The terns were finding a way to use it. Each of the other

summers the male had spent here, the shelf-ice had drifted away soon after the river broke up. The ice had come loose from the shore, then had split into large and small rafts which sailed out to the Bering Sea, where they followed the Bering Sea floes up into the Arctic Ocean. But this year the shelf-ice already had blown away once and come back. When it returned, on a flood tide, it was cast up on the beach so high that it never again floated free. As the top surface melted, the sea spread across it. Some of the cakes of river ice scattered over the drowned shelf-ice and became stranded there. They were of fantastic shapes, for the currents that drained through the river had thawed out intricate paths in its frozen channel. The eery and iridescent ice masses were like domiciles in a fairy tale. In them the tern had found a few archways and alcoves where he could perch, unseen by the jaegers, and make a quick dive for a passing fish.

For those few opportunities the tern stayed on this coast. They kept him alive, but they did not allow his romance to progress. Only here in Alaska, only by rearing a brood together, could a permanent bond between him and a new mate be established. And must he leave the North for the fourth time with a sense of completion missed?

He never had been a destroyer of eggs when he could get fish, but, being so often hungry, the tern looked with increasing interest at the many jaegers' nests on the mossier parts of the marsh. He did not glimpse the olive-brown spotted eggs many times, for the jaeger parents changed guard without often leaving the nests alone; yet the fact of the eggs being there was a nagging knowledge. In coursing about, seeking moths and mosquitoes, the tern had discovered where all the nests were, several hundred of them.

So far they were unmolested. In most years the Eskimos did not bother to hunt for jaegers' eggs. They prized them, but there were too few to make searching worth while. One morning however, as if the Eskimos suddenly realized what an opportunity they were missing, they began scattering out over the marsh. They quartered across it, frequently stopping to pick up the eggs and put them into their parka pockets.

The jaegers were greatly excited. The hens had always been clever at luring a human away from a nest. Sometimes the bird, inconspicuously leaving the eggs, would tumble along the ground, as if with a broken wing. She hoped that the hunter would try to catch her; when she had led him away from the nest, she would fly up and be gone. The Eskimos knew that strategy and did not often pursue the hens. Therefore the hens tried a different trick. Stealing away through the grass unseen, one would take to the wing and fly only a little distance. She would settle down onto the ground again, arranging herself cozily on a mossy tussock, as if she were covering eggs. When the Eskimo had approached her there, she would repeat the performance. The egg-hunters knew that some of the time they were being fooled, and yet they followed the hens, because their best means of locating the eggs had always been just that: of watching for an alighting bird.

The villagers' searching meant that the meadow was full of unguarded eggs—a fabulous opportunity and the break in the tern's bad luck. Since he knew where the nests were, he soared near the Eskimos as they searched, and when a hen left her nest to delude the human, the tern would dip over it and, with practiced speed, scoop the eggs into his bill. If an incoming jaeger cock saw him and attacked, the tern simply broke the eggs and spewed them out. As he flew about, the jaeger hens would look up at him with indignant eyes: they had sensed his intentions. When a human hunter came near however, the instinctive fear was strong, and the hen always left the nest.

A few of the other terns, including his young companion, were imitating the male in his happy discovery. Indeed it was through the terns' help that the humans found most of the nests. Once knowing where they were, the Eskimos came back to them on succeeding days. With the terns' willing assistance, they took the second, third, and fourth clutches the jaegers laid. Scarcely one jaeger pair was incubating an undisturbed nest.

Before long, then, some of the nests were deserted. Where were the adult birds? Soon the facts were apparent: the majority of the jaegers were going home to their original nesting grounds; discouraged here, they returned to the rivers and beaches that they had left to follow the lemmings. Each day their numbers were smaller on Norton Sound.

Being well fed and at peace, the male tern and the female were spending much of the time at the homesite beside Grassy Lake. The courtship again was progressing. Several times they performed a ritual in which one bird circled the other, frequently bowing, after which they changed places. Next the male scraped out three or four hollows among the pebbles. The female chose one of the little depressions and deepened it. While she rested upon it, the male picked up bits of twigs, grass, and leaves, and tossed them in her direction. She gathered them in with her bill and arranged the material in a rim around her. The time had come then for their last, lyrical preliminary of love.

It took place on a warm, still morning after all the jaegers had left except those that had migrated north with the flock. The tern and the female had been foraging and had caught several fish apiece. Neither was hungry, but when she went back to the nest, the male followed her with a capelin, this one a gift. She begged for it and when he presented it, took it gracefully, laying it on the edge of the nest.

A cobweb of clouds was spread over the earth, except near the green-gold horizon. There in the translucent air, images of the offshore ice, pearly reflections, mirages, hung motionless. The wind was quiet, and all voices seemed hushed in relief from the recent conflicts. The male tern left the nest and, sweeping away toward the mountains, started soaring into the sky. Instinct prompted the female. She followed, beginning her rise from the opposite side of the marsh. The two continued on up, widely separated, through the clouds into the privacy of an altitude above all other birds. There in the sunlight they swung toward each other, coming together until they were close enough for a wing-touch.

Oblivious then to everything but the ecstasy of shared movement, they began a long, breathless glide to the earth. They were performing an aerial dance as they dropped, a darting, swinging descent in which they constantly passed and repassed each other. Approaching the clouds, they entered the mist and came out of it without knowing, sensing only their rapture.

Now the sea's crinkled surface had become visible as waves, the berry bushes were seen separately, and the birds could distinguish their nest from the pebbles and twigs surrounding it. Banking together, the fall checked, the pair circled

Grassy Lake. They alighted under the edge of the willows and there completed their union.

By the aerial glide they had woven a bond between them, and many times it would be renewed. It was a bond as strong as their flight and as delicate.

CHAPTER 7

The Hunters Are the Hunted

The morning was mild in its start, with the beluga female, in company with the rest of the herd of whales, loafing along the fringe of the ice. The ice field was moving up toward the arctic. Through the winter the ice had covered the Bering Sea, south to Alaska's Bristol Bay and across to Siberia's Cape Olyutorskiy. The beluga whales had been spending those months, with the walrus and bearded seals, in the loose drift of broken cakes at the edge. Food was plentiful there, and no enemies bothered them, no killer whales and no Eskimos. Late in May, then, southerly winds and currents began to push the whole ice pack northward. The walrus would go with it on up through Bering Strait, but the whales and the seals would leave it. They had stayed with the ice, however, until that June morning when, having traveled two hundred miles, they were opposite Norton Sound. And they still were idling among the white ice cakes and floes that sparkled along the blue water. The water was quiet. Smooth glossy welts of motion slid over it but no foaming waves. In the depths where the female was resting the sound of the passing swells was a whisper that rose and fell like the breath of a creature asleep. The rhythm well matched her mood, which was drowsy and indolent.

Every ten minutes or so, whenever she needed fresh oxygen in her lungs, she would fan her tail just enough to propel her up to the surface. It was a trifling effort because in effect she weighed nothing, she was as buoyant, everywhere that she swam, as if the sea canceled gravity. After she took a new breath she would drift down again, to hang in the water with trancelike stillness, though her eyes followed the walrus diving for clams and the fish weaving their webs of bubbles around her. She came wider awake when one of the big male seals vaulted out of the water and threw himself onto an ice cake. By then, with the summer progressing, the smaller cakes were no more than ice skeletons, and the one he had mounted collapsed, dropping the seal in a puddle of chilly mush.

A young whale, a yearling, came nudging along the beluga's side. The touch was a greeting, for she was his voluntary, devoted nurse. The maternal instinct was so well developed in white whales that most of those without young assisted the mothers of offspring. This little whale was the female's particular charge. All through the winter she had been helping to guard him. She was spending less time with him now that she soon would have one of her own, but she still felt some responsibility for him.

That morning his mother was with him but was not giving him much attention. She was entertaining herself by teasing a fish. Dropping a piece of squid in front of a pollock, she would turn aside till the fish moved forward to take the food, when she would whirl around quickly and snap it up. She baited the pollock again and again, and he continued to let her fool him. Tired of the game then, she ate the pollock and swam off among the white hideaways under the ice. The yearling remained with his foster mother. He himself played with a fish, a tomcod, catching it, letting it go, cat-and-mouse fun, and she watched him. When he too had eaten his fish, he headed out into the open water. He was almost old enough to look after himself; yet she felt slightly distressed at his daring.

Swayed by the undulant stir of the sea, the beluga eased off to sleep again. She lay with her head and tail drooping, suspended so heavily that she looked as if she could be roused by nothing less than a tempest, or the young life within her becoming impatient, finally, for its birth. But it was something quite small, indistinct at first, that caused her to open her eyes and straighten herself for a quick dash-away. It was a faint but different beat in an ocean already full of rhythm, of the accented motions of waves and of swimming animals.

The white whale was warily quiet now . . . listening . . . trying to catch over all of her smooth rounded body this change in the usual sounds of her element. Sounds in the sea were more than external evidence caught by one's ears. They were actual thrusts of the water, felt anywhere on one's skin.

Unmistakably there was a new vibration.

From the south, a wide thrashing. Belugas themselves churned up the water like that when they swam as a herd. But these splashes were fluctuating. At regular intervals they were breaking in noisy cascades. The climax was timed so perfectly that it seemed practiced, deliberate. For the pulse was the onward driving of killer whales, a band of them swimming in close formation, all slicing up out of the surface together and rolling down under as one. And they were, in fact, one—united in a most terrible purpose.

With a quick smooth glide the beluga began to swing toward the ice, and a refuge. But her escape was checked by alarm for the little whale. He had gone out in the ocean, away from a shelter. And was he still there, with the threat of the killers advancing?

The female turned into the danger. Since the water was roily, she could not see very far, but she listened now for some sign that the small whale was swimming near. And she called in a low urgent voice, sending her summons out to him through the water. The splash of the killers approaching was louder, and that could confuse him. She continued to search. But she needed a breath! She rose cautiously, only dipping her blowhole up into the air, gasping a new lungful, and slipping below the surface, and down, and down.

The sea was now quiet except for the killers' movement. The walrus and seals, as well as the whales, had fled into the niches beneath the ice. Finally, when to stay in the killers' path would mean almost sure capture, the female sped back to safety. She entered the ice area with relief, under a surface mottled with slush and then under larger cakes, inverted mounds hung from the top of the water. Concealed in a hollow between two of these she discovered the yearling, huddled beside his mother. The female went farther, down lanes of water between the large floes, not stopping until she had reached an ice grotto she knew in the wall of the solid ice field. All glistening white herself, like a phantom of the far North, she was hidden as well in that frosty nook as a dark-furred animal is in the forest. The white labyrinth of the ice was her camouflage, and instinctively there she relaxed.

This was the killers' first reappearance after a winter spent in warm southern waters. There their young had been born and the adults held their mating carnivals. Most of the killers that journeyed north every spring would remain along the Aleutian Islands, where they found victims such as the larger whales, and the fur seals bound for their breeding grounds on the Pribilof Islands, not far away in the Bering Sea. That was an opportunity that detained some of the killers. But others came on, into the colder waters, themselves. Twenty-seven were in this band that now had progressed to the ice.

The killers' arrival completed a food chain of which the belugas were one of the center links. According to nature's heartless but practical plan, every animal in the chain was both hunter and hunted. At one end were the tiny and help-less travelers of the plankton. The ocean currents had washed them into a dense concentration there at the edge of the ice. Those first links in the chain were indeed very fine, creatures too small to be seen by the human eye, feeding on others still more minute—but the fish had found them.

The plankton animals were the food of the little fish, which in turn became food for the larger species of their own kind. Then the white whales ate any fish of sufficient size to nour-ish a creature of twelve-foot length. Other sorts of whales, curiously the largest ones, had baleen plates in their mouths with which they could strain out the plankton, but the be-lugas had only teeth. During the eight winter months, in the community there in the loose drift of ice, the chain stopped with the belugas. For they had no enemies in that season. But late in the spring two more links were added, men and killer whales. Both tried to capture belugas and men, too, were sometimes the victims of killers. By then, in June, the whole contest was being transferred to the waters along the coast. The fish were leaving the deeper parts of the ocean, seeking the rivers and beaches to spawn, and the white whales would follow them. They had no other choice, even though the fish took them into the range of the Eskimos' harpoons and guns.

The killers had come, the safe season had ended. Swiftly however, the menacing rhythm died out of the placid currents along the ice. The female came out from the floes, to the open sea where two other belugas already were playing catch with a cod, and a walrus was teaching her young one how to submerge. The white whale was by now uncomfortable, since the recent excitement had tripped the expected event in her life. Not yet in much pain however, she swam back and forth, near the walrus.

While the walrus calf, about a month old, was swimming along the surface, the mother would come up behind him and placing her tusks on his shoulders would force him down. At the touch on his back he would take a deep breath and the two would descend together, nine or ten fathoms, to the dark, level expanse of the ocean floor there, where, if the calf were not needing air badly, the mother would scrape up some shellfish. Two years would pass before the young walrus' tusks would be long enough for him to get his own clams, but the sea was his element and he should be at home in it. Sometimes between dives he climbed out on an ice cake, but his mother would not allow him to rest there long.

The beluga had been amusing herself by swimming around the pair, but soon she ignored them, for her suffering was acute. She slid along past the under surfaces of the ice, often hitting it with her forehead. That was her method of breaking the ice to breathe when it was thin; now she was only trying to counteract one agony with another. A few times she threw herself up on the edge of a cake, scraping her belly upon it as she sank into the waves again.

The birth took about thirty minutes. Her little one's tail, the wide fans of his flukes, which were limp and soft, appeared first, in the normal way. For a while then there was trouble. On his sides were his paddle-shaped fins, and one of them caught. At this stage however the fin, like the flukes, lacked the stiffening it would later have, and before long it slipped out. The mother whale turned around with a characteristic quick fling of her body that snapped the umbilical cord. Then she hastily boosted her young one up to the surface for air. With his head out of the water he took his first breath and squealed, a sound half a gasp and half whistle. She answered him with a warm, gentle note, after which she swam under him. He instinctively took his place at one side of the low ridge on her back. For the next few months that would be the position in which he would accompany her.

In spite of the floppiness of his fins and flukes, which would not become firm for about two weeks, he could swim almost as fast as his mother could. He was very precocious. To that end nature had had his mother's pregnancy last for eleven months, whereas animals such as foxes, that simply lie in a den when they are first born, are carried a shorter time. The young whale was further developed than fox cubs and he also, like other whales, had a superior mind. It was much more complex than a fox's.

For the next few hours, in order to keep him safe, the mother stayed in the leads of water between the floes. Once when they rose for a breath she swung off to the side to see his enchanting smallness, not four feet long, and his infant face. He had wide-spaced eyes, full lips, and a prominent forehead, his being due to a pad of fat but its profile was like a human's. His ears were but tiny canals, needing no shells of cartilage to catch sounds in the water. On top of his head was his blowhole, navel-shaped and closed tightly except when he took a new breath.

His hairless skin was the ocean's own color, gray with a tint of green-blue. This was the first spring that his mother, now four years old, had attained the smooth, gleaming whiteness of an adult beluga. There was not one mark of color upon her; even her tongue was white, and she was a lovely thing to see, appearing so pure, so immaculate, in the dark shining water. But to her the gray infant was the more beautiful.

With a motion that was a summons, meaning that he should come, the mother slid under the young whale again and dived. Wherever she turned, he was touching her. But as if the touch were not contact enough, they kept reaching out to each other with sounds. The mother's vocabulary was quite extensive. She had little soft barks, a low warning note, and calls that any creature could recognize as affectionate. Often her voice had a musical, bell-like quality, and usually a wistfulness. They were wild sounds but with a tone that seemed slightly sad.

As she cruised through the ice with her son, she could hear that the walrus was exercising her calf again. The belugas, the seals, and the walrus all had their typical ways of swimming; the whale could distinguish among them. She was listening to the walrus, out in the flow of the tide, when suddenly she was catching again the dreaded vibration. She

hung in the depths between two cakes of ice, hidden, motionless, with her son just above her back. The sound in the
sea became more distinct, its crescendo more definite. It could
be only the killers returning. Mingled with it, now, was a
violent splashing as walrus mother and calf tried to reach
the ice.

The calf had climbed onto his mother's shoulders but she
was not able to save him. The tall swordlike fins of the killers
drew near too fast, cleaving the water, rolling up, over, and
down all in unison. One of the killers had dived under the
parent walrus. He rose, striking her chest with a blow so powerful that the calf was thrown several feet in the air and off
to the side. When he fell back in the water he disappeared
into the gaping mouth of the killer, with its great pointed
teeth. The mother pursued the attacker. Bellowing in her
rage, she held up her head with her tusks, two feet long and
sharp, ready to make their strike. The killer escaped however,
for he could swim faster than she. His thirty-foot length,
glistening black with white ovals behind the eyes, made a
last arrogant leap, clearing the surface. With the rest of the
band, then, he left. As far as they could be seen the black
rapiers swung up out of the water and down with a perfect
rhythm.

The walrus heaved herself onto the ice, where she lay roaring with anger and grief, and with pain, for the killer had
bruised her chest. If she had been a beluga the blow would
have meant her death, but the ribs of the walrus were padded
with thicker blubber. Several times the white whale had seen
members of her own herd struck from below by killers. Their
bones were broken, even their hearts were crushed, before
they were hurled from the water. They never knew when

they fell in the waves again, and the killer pack gathered around to share the grim celebration. The killers ate only the inner flesh. The white skin and the fibrous fat, torn off in sheets, drifted to shore where the Eskimos salvaged it.

"He share with me!" an Eskimo always cried when he saw a killer attack a beluga. "Strong, brave killer whale," the Eskimo often added, meanwhile paddling as fast as possible toward the beach. The praise was meant to appease the spirits of killers, for men greatly feared them.

The killer band had apparently gone to some other part of the Bering Sea. After several hours had passed with no sign of them, the mother beluga was reassured and began showing her son the fine points of whale swimming. She was as light in her motions as one of the gulls would have been if it could float in the air, all its energy used to propel itself, and it was one of the whale's real pleasures to glide about with her buoyant and streamlined body at rest in the water. While the infant stayed close to her back, she taught him some of a whale's supple turns, banks, and barrel rolls.

Within two or three days he was ready to make the trip to the coast. The mother was anxious to go, for fish were becoming scarce here along the ice, and she needed more food with the young one to nurse. They set out about midnight. The ice field dwindled out, ended thirty miles from the land, a long distance without any refuge if the killer whales should return. The beluga maintained as fast a speed as her son could keep up. When she no longer could feel his touch, she would wait for him and then stop and give him some milk, but she did not allow him to dawdle. Toward morning they came to the sandbars and islands that fanned out in the sea off the Yukon delta.

Here again they were safe from the killers, which never went into shallow waters where they could not submerge the fins on their backs, six feet tall on the older males. Belugas, being but half as large and built more compactly, were satisfied if the water was deep enough so that they could make headway. In one of the river's channels was plenty of flow to grip with one's tail, while everywhere off at the sides spread an expanse of liquid meadows. In them the mother and son would be safe from killers.

The herring run had commenced. The dark blue-green hordes were striping the water with their own currents. They were so numerous that the whales seemed to swim in a sea of fish. The mother had not paused to catch any food on the journey across from the ice. She was hungry, and now she ate several of the herring. Her son seemed bewildered by all the activity that surrounded him.

The ice in the Yukon had gone out so recently that the trash it brought down still floated about in the waves and was strewn on the beaches. Spruce trees and cottonwoods, that had stood on the riverbanks more than a thousand miles inland only a few weeks earlier, had been undercut by the ice. Now they lay in the sea, their foliage and roots awash. The female herring were swarming around them. They always tried to deposit their sticky eggs on some object, such as driftwood or reeds, to which they would adhere till they hatched. As the females pressed into the tops of the prostrate trees, the males were among them, in such numbers that the water around the herring was opaque with the milt.

For a while the belugas swam about lazily in the lee of one of the sandbars. The morning was wide and clean over the water, which was everywhere twinkling with sunlit ripples.

The darling new little whale was alive and well and for the time being safe. The herring would continue to stream up the coast for a week or more, and after them would come other great schools of fish, smelts and salmon. The gifts of nature seemed bountiful on that day.

But the whales, like the fish, had a schedule. In two or three weeks they would be due off the arctic coast. There the herd reassembled. During the northward journey they often dispersed, but they came together again near Point Hope, where the courtships took place. The summer was spent in those far-Northern waters, after which the belugas turned south, a few days ahead of the ice. They moved then as a group, swimming in V-formation, wherefore the Eskimos called them geese of the sea. It was time for the mother and son to start on their way to Point Hope to meet them.

At the protruding corner where the coast made its right-angle swing into Norton Sound was St. Michael, an Eskimo settlement. The beluga remembered it. As they passed it, she and the infant would turn farther out in the ocean; such was the white whales' habit when they approached any village.

She did not turn out soon enough. As they rounded a moss-covered bank on the shore, an Eskimo darted out from the cove beyond in his kayak. His harpoon was flung from upraised hand. The whales were then at the surface, having risen to breathe, and the head of the harpoon struck the infant in one of his shoulders.

Tied to the pointed tip was a very long rope of walrus hide. The sharp ivory tip was so designed that it came out of the shaft when it struck, but it continued to trail the rope. At the other end of the rope was a float, a poke, as the Eskimos called it. The poke was a sealskin with all of its openings sewed up tight, and the skin inflated with air. Wherever the whales might swim, now, that seal would follow them on the surface. And the hunter would follow the seal.

The mother whale raced away from the land with the infant still close to her back. In her alarm, however, she swam too fast and was drawing away from him. She found him again, and afterwards kept her speed down to his, meanwhile coaxing him on with tense, urgent calls.

Since the infant could not hold his breath for longer than five or six minutes, in each mile of their flight they would have to risk being seen. They were but a short way ahead of the boat when the young whale swam up to the top. He did not yet know how to make a smooth rise, as his mother did; she could catch a new breath and show only her blowhole and a low line behind it, but all the forepart of his body shot out of the surface. The man fired—his bullets were quick white nicks in the water surrounding the whales. But being so dark the small whale was not a conspicuous target. This time the hunter had missed.

The mother made a deep dive, guiding her young one down close to the ocean floor. She was trying instinctively to avoid being seen, not understanding that the sealskin would make it impossible to conceal their course from the Eskimo. The seal, bouncing along on the waves, jerked the rope, causing each time a new stab of pain in the infant's flesh. A harder tug would have pulled the harpoon point out of his shoulder, giving the pair a chance to elude the man, but the point was securely lodged and the float was not catching on anything. The small whale swam steadily and as fast as he could. He was touching his mother through most of his length, clinging to her but driving himself as hard as if he had known that this was not one of the normal problems, in which one would turn to a mother for help. He was the one that must free himself of the rope.

When the mother could feel that he needed a breath, by the convulsiveness of his motions, she lifted him by her own ascent. They emerged from the water and bullets again splashed around them. The waves aided them. There in the Sound they were high enough to be breaking in white caps, and they made it difficult for the man to take steady aim.

The mother was starting to comprehend that this chase was different from others—that a headlong flight out to sea would not take them to safety, for the hunter would stay behind them. Her fear, for her small son more than herself, was now tending toward panic. She would try a new stratagem. Back of the coastline here was a wide low area where tidal sloughs, channels and bays, wound intricately through the tundra. One could enter the mouth of a stream and beyond could disappear in a maze of water and islands with banks of wet reeds. On another year she had escaped from a hunter there.

When the whales dived again she made a sharp turn and headed in toward the shore. The rope became slack as they doubled upon their course, but it caught with a tug when the sealskin was picked up again. The pair had to rise for one other breath, but finally they entered the mouth of the stream and the marsh. The mother's anxiety eased. It seemed to her, as they glided through numerous bays, opening one from another, that surely the hunter had lost them.

They reached a last, remote channel where the mother felt that they were well hidden and there she stopped. The infant was very tired. She gave him some milk, a nursing which took place under water and lasted not more than ten seconds, for the bladderlike reservoirs of her mammary glands were completely filled. The little whale's lips and cheeks had no muscles, therefore he could not suck, but as soon as he took her teat she, by a contraction, ejected a stream of milk into his mouth. It was as rich as the thickest cream. In rapid succession she fed him several more times, and then for a while the two rested, submerged in the water and coming up for a breath, when they needed one, so drowsily that they scarcely knew.

At the time they entered the sloughs, the tide was still short of its crest. As it continued to rise, the sealskin drifted beyond the whales. Later it floated past them again, drawn by the receding water back toward the river's mouth. The whales, sleeping heavily, were not aware of the change in the flow, but once when the mother was letting herself sink down from the surface, the flukes of her tail touched the bottom too soon. She swung the tail and came quickly awake. She realized that the tide was going out, rapidly now. They could not remain here any longer.

She and her infant moved toward the beach again. As they were crossing a sandbar she found the water so shallow that she must turn on her side, swinging her flukes horizontally, to get over. At the outer reed beds they stayed for a brief time while the mother fed on the herring that were depositing eggs on the stalks. And then the belugas proceeded out into the sea.

As they were drawing away from the shore they saw the long, slim, white shape of the hunter's kayak above them. They saw the anchor snatched up and the Eskimo's paddle make its first dip. He had known of the possibility that he could lose the whales while they were in the marsh. He also knew that the fall of the tide would force the pair to come out again. He therefore had let down his anchor and waited outside the stream.

The chase was resumed. It seemed hopeless indeed, but the whales could not simply allow themselves to be taken. Now in late afternoon the waves were subsiding, and when the belugas emerged from the water they found that the hunter's bullets were striking closer. He was trying to hit either whale. He wanted the mother but his experience with belugas told him that if he should kill the infant she would not leave its body. This opportunity was important to him. He too had a young one, a child that was sick, and the only food in his cabin was fish. A change from that diet to one of the tender white skin of beluga would hasten the child's recovery, he thought. He was not killing for sport; here on this northwest coast of Alaska the food chains of nature still included the human race—this was one of the few places left on earth where that was true. Elsewhere, by growing cattle and crops, most men had removed themselves from the succession of lives that prey on other free lives, but the Eskimos occupied an eternally frozen country, which would not grow harvests nor planned pasturage. Animals were not killed for pleasure, but they were in all the more danger because their pursuers, human as well as wild, were motivated by hunger.

The contest between the beluga and man was one parent's skill against that of another, and the mother's next move was to take her young one out toward Egg Island, a steep mound of rock on whose crags kittiwake and murre colonies nested. She did not know what she would do when they arrived

there, but at least she and the infant would not be exposed on the whole wide stretch of the sea.

As they approached the island the mother swam to the side where, as she remembered, the cliffs formed a bay. Would the bay, like the sloughs, be a hiding place? She still did not understand why this hunter could not be evaded. It was evident by this time that something about the chase was not right. The normal relationship between hunter and hunted was not in effect, for none of the usual ruses was working—not the dodging, or the long, motionless wait on the ocean floor, the rapid flight, or the blending of one's white self with the white curls on the ridges of waves. These methods, instinctive with the whale's species, were here, amazingly, of no use, and the mother was now both confused and desperate. But she felt some relief as she entered the bay, where the water was deep and quiet. The whales dived to the bottom and rested there.

Birds, a large congregation of them, were swimming about on the surface. That in itself, the birds' lack of alarm, gave the beluga confidence. Nothing was seen of the murres from below but their bellies, white exactly to waterline, and the pink legs that were pushing the melon-shaped bellies about. Sometimes one murre chased another, but most merely were idling. One bird had dived. Using his wings to propel him, he went all the way to the floor of the bay. There he found a small pebble and brought it back to the top in his slender bill. He let it fall, dived after it, took it up, dropped it. For several minutes he played with his pretty stone. And a kittiwake skated down onto the surface. The dainty webs broke through first and then the white breast. The bird trod the water, flapping his wings until he was upright, only his toes submerged.

After he settled himself in a floating position there was no more disturbance. The murres swam about lazily, and the heart of the mother whale slowed to its normal pace.

The placidness of the sea made it possible for her to hear the killer whales when they were still a fair distance away. The crashing, the flat metallic din when the water was slapped by so many dives, fast became louder. The killers were entering Norton Sound. If they should pass near the island they could discover the mother and infant. With all of her body she reached for the clatter, trying to sense its direction.

For several minutes now there had been no sign of the man. His boat was not visible on the surface above the white whales, nor was the sealskin. The rope from the harpoon head trailed out behind the cliff . . . but it was slackening. The float was drifting, apparently, closer in toward the belugas.

The kayak came suddenly leaping along the surface around the cliff. Very fast were the dips of the Eskimo's paddle. Had he seen the killers and was he seeking a place to land? Or had he glimpsed the pale forms below on the ocean floor? He stopped near the rocks at the beach, where he kept his place by adroit turns of his paddle. It was a short-handled paddle, held under the kayak, not out at the side, in the hope that the whales would mistake the boat for a drifting log. The mother knew better. During the moment when she first heard the killers her fear of them banished her consciousness of the man. Now she had two different terrors to balance.

As the hunter appeared in the bay, all the birds had splashed up into flight. Soon the water was smooth again. Only the beat of the killers' approach broke the submarine silence. The route of the killers was evident. They were coming east, into the Sound, and would cross the channel between the coast and the island. The mother must act. The air in the white whales' lungs was not quite exhausted, but it was getting short. She must choose between enemies—the killers, which hunted in well-known ways, traditional in the sea, and this human whose method was mystifying and so infallible. If the belugas had only not needed to breathe, they might have waited here till the killers were gone; then the mother again would have attempted to dash away from the Eskimo. But if they stayed, in a very short time they must rise to the surface in range of his gun.

The killers, her instinct said, probably were the lesser danger. If she and her son could hold their breaths enough longer to swim to the shore, the wild predators would not follow them into the shallows. The killers might catch them en route, but if they stayed close to the bottom the killers, cutting along through the top of the water, could miss them. They had a chance to escape from the killers, but none to escape from the man.

Faster than thought the mother set out, and the infant, alert to the danger, responded as if he were part of her body. They swam at their best speed, with the little whale driving himself frantically to keep up with his mother. They had not yet been found, but the killers were very close. Unexpectedly then, with a rip of flesh, the head of the harpoon was torn from the infant's shoulder. The killers had seen the seal, racing along the surface, and closed on it. One of them tossed it aloft for a sporting catch and in doing so jerked the rope with sufficient force to pull out the point. The small whale was freed.

The belugas did reach the safe waters along the coast. For

the attack on the sealskin had distracted the entire pack of killers. The one that had gulped the inflated skin swung his head angrily as the punctured float burst in his mouth. The band milled about for a while, sensing that possible victims were in the sea here, but finally they assembled themselves again and moved away in formation, farther into the Sound.

In the breakers along the shore the belugas themselves advanced eastward, inaccessible to the killers and lost to the hunter. Beyond was a lonely land where they would not soon be encountering men again. After an hour or so the mother allowed herself to play with her young one, rolling him over and over and talking to him with small and endearing sounds.

CHAPTER 8

The Honorable Death
of a Rogue

The previous days had been desperate. Towering mounds of ice had been crashing around the rogue walrus as a storm from the Bering Sea, whipping up toward the North Pole, had fractured the arctic pack into separate floes. During the winter the ice had been frozen into a nearly continuous field. With the spring's advance the cover of snow, melting, ran into cracks and made it possible for the pounding winds to split up the pack. The floes were of iceberg size, with ridges extending skyward fifty and sixty feet and with bases under the surface several times as deep. The gale tossed them about like rudderless ships, driving one into another. To survive the chaos the walrus had had to be active, to stay awake for several days and nights, and by the storm's end he had been exhausted. Climbing onto an ice cake, he had had a long sleep. Now he was awake, enjoying the warmth of the sun on his belly and seeing in every direction the new, open lanes of water through which he could leave this realm of eternal ice between Wrangel Island and the northern Siberian coast.

Through them he would be able to go to his summering grounds off the coast of Alaska, where he would find the great walrus herds from the Bering Sea. There perhaps old and aching desires might be fulfilled; there his long lonely years might come to a happier ending.

The air, even now, was stirred by the storm's trailing gusts, but these were not lifting the water. Its surface was placid, stilled by the tall structures of sapphire-blue ice. The floes had spread out on the sea, enclosing small intimate chambers and stately courtyards that opened one into another, more splendid than marble halls human beings have dreamt of. All were floored by the polished water, and sheets of prismatic colors shimmered from water to crystal walls. The sky overhead was a cloudless dome of blue light.

The walrus' hind flippers spread to the sides, relaxed; his foreflippers were idly scratching. With the back of his head on the ice, the two sharp white tusks, that grew to a length of ten inches out of his mouth, pointed skyward, as did the bristles that covered his upper lip. They were bristles thicker than porcupine quills, and he viewed the world through their mesh. He was able to see all about him because his eyes, though not large, had a mobility almost like those of a lobster.

He was watching a flock of fulmars and gulls that were soaring about in the air, waiting for him to start hunting. Crumbs from his meal would furnish their nourishment; meanwhile they scanned the water for shellfish, capelin, shrimps, any morsels of life that might show themselves. The sun, shining through the translucent white wings, drew outlines around the birds' curving sides.

Summer and sun and movement—these had presented themselves all at once on that day, which was June twenty-second.

But even then, as the walrus' eyes followed the gulls, out of the north appeared a long, undulating line of ducks traveling in single file. They were Pacific eiders, the males, leaving their mates in the nests on Wrangel's low treeless hills. Birds flying south: a reminder that the sweet season would not be long. On the journey the walrus would soon undertake, he would see life everywhere, on the coast, in the skies, in the seas. But within a few weeks all the migrating flocks and their young, most of the fish, the whales, and the other walrus would have deserted the arctic. The polar bears, the white foxes, and some of the seals would remain, but these would be scattered. Days would pass in which the rogue would have no glimpse of a living creature. He would try, meanwhile, to repair his desolate state, but he had little time. So warned the banner of ducks, rippling away through the sky, the first sign of autumn, now on the opening day of summer.

He rolled himself onto his side, more than a ton of flesh, and reared his head, like the peak of a pyramid over the massive and spreading girth of his chest. If seals were not here in these leads of water, the rogue must seek them, today, before he proceeded eastward, for he had not had any food since the start of the storm. Hooking his tusks in the ice, pulling himself along while he pushed with his fanned-out flippers, he came to the edge of his floe. As he dived he seemed almost as boneless as a gigantic snail; yet his tumble was not without grace. The ice, relieved of his weight, rose two feet.

He swam with smooth, noiseless strokes, his flippers able to move more freely than those of seals. The gulls accompanied him. They would advise his prey that he was coming, but he could not disperse the birds nor could he hide from them. Even though he was submerged most of the time, he would be visible to them, below in the clear arctic sea, and they also could follow him by the strings of bubbles.

All winter seals had been here, able to breathe through the holes in the ice they had made—a skill not possessed by the rogue. Through what cracks he could find, he had gone below and had captured enough prey to live, though not to live well; his foraging had not been easy.

Where now were those seals? He soon heard a promising pulse in the sea, steady and rhythmical. He approached it cautiously and, a few feet under the surface, discovered a small seal absorbed in chasing its tail. Till the gleaming and murderous tusks were upon him the seal did not notice the rogue. But the seal's hind flippers instantly clapped sole to sole and, used as a rudder-propeller, shot him out of sight into a cavern below the ice.

The walrus pursued him. The cavern opened into a spacious area between floes, where the chase became faster. Sometimes the two were in uncluttered channels, sometimes under the ice, in and out of the shadows. The seal was not only quick; he was adroit at swinging around the turns and the cornices, difficult for so large an animal as the rogue . . . and yet it was curious that the walrus had not succeeded in catching him. This was something new, that a seal so young could escape. The rogue drove himself. But his body was not streamlined; it was formed, with its bulk at the shoulders, to hold him head-down in the water, and not for speed. And if the rogue's life had been normal, he would not have attempted to catch any prey so swift. Now in a straight stretch the seal drew away from him. It was disconcerting, even alarming, that the walrus could not overtake such an immature victim; yet he gave up the effort. Much winded he hung at the surface, only his nostrils out, panting, needing another rest so soon after loafing upon the ice cake.

The chase had taken the walrus southward. He was in thinner ice now, not blue like the older floes but green-silver. When he recovered, he swam ahead in the same direction and entered a loose white drift, pans and cakes frothy and porous. This was the kind of ice where the seals, basking on top, often could be surprised.

But it was not the scent of his usual prey that soon startled him; it was the scent of a human—man, eater of walrus flesh. Up went the rogue's tusks, instinctively, to the attacking position. New strength seemed to surge through his muscles. He was a walrus again in his prime, filled with a blinding compulsion to slaughter.

The man was evidently an Eskimo, for his own scent was mingled with those of his sealskin boots and caribou parka with wolverine ruff. Combined with them too was that of a freshly killed ribbon seal but the rogue scarcely perceived it; his fury was even more stimulating than hunger. He was approaching the long, nearly straight edge of the shelf-ice attached to the shores of Siberia. If the man should be up on that ice plateau, the rogue could not reach him. But he would soon know.

He had seen the Eskimo several minutes before the man, who had not smelled the walrus, was conscious that he was coming. The man knelt on an ice pan beside the seal, which was dead. He had ridden his dog sled from shore to the brink of the shelf-ice to hunt and had shot the seal in the water. Leaving his gun on the sled he had gone out to retrieve his seal, using the small pan of ice as a raft and propelling it with a paddle, a *lukzoon* tied onto his spear.

The walrus swam into the lane of water between the man's raft and the shelf-ice. The man had seen him. He froze, wary as any wild animal. In his heightened odor the rogue could detect emotion, but the man was showing no other sign of fear as he watched the great beast that was cutting off his escape. The Eskimo had removed the paddle from his harpoon and now held the spear. Staying out of its range, the walrus reared until his immense chest was out of the water. He was roaring and bellowing, flinging his head back and then suddenly jabbing it forward, a motion impulsively born of his wish. He charged along a few feet and repeated the threat. He could dive, come up from beneath and upset the floe and then, grasping the human between his foreflippers, he could attack with his tusks. Any moment he chose he could do that, but he was not ready yet. He was controlling the situation entirely, and he would prolong the pleasure.

He had more reason, actually, than he knew to resent a man, but he knew enough. Even if he could not remember as far back as his infancy, he had had recent encounters with human beings. Hunters had speared him and shot at him; he was carrying several of their bullets under his skin. But their greatest injury to him he could not comprehend.

The happening had occurred when he was but two months old, migrating north with a devoted mother and a protective father. The time, then too, had been June and his family, with numerous others, had relaxed on a wide field of ice while the ice transported them without effort over the sun-bejeweled length of the Bering Sea. A thousand-mile trip lay ahead of them; meanwhile the mothers were nursing their young, the other females were being courted, and all sang as they sailed along, enjoying the sway of the ice, its momentum over the waves that splashed on the edge of the field. After the Yukon delta was passed, and Cape Nome, they came to Sledge Island and the sheer cliffs of King Island where thousands of gulls, kittiwakes, and murres wheeled out from their nests at the sight of the herd.

The older walrus knew where the clam beds were, and when the ice moved along over them, some would dive down to the floor of the sea, to rake their pairs of long canine teeth into the mud for the shellfish. They worked rapidly, for the ice was sailing away at a pace of better than twenty-five yards a minute, and none dared to be left far behind. Walrus had died of exhaustion in trying to overtake ice that had gone too far ahead of them. And so, when the little one's parents had left him to forage, they never were gone very long, and he did not dive down to the beds himself, for he would not be able to do any digging until he was two years old. His tusks would not have grown out until then, and in the interval he should be nursed.

The sociable herd had been able to stay together as far as the bottleneck of the Bering Strait. There a wind from the north had broken their field of ice into many small floes. The walrus that rode on them would be separated but briefly. Within two or three days they could expect the current to take them all in the same direction, to Point Hope and on to Icy Cape on the arctic coast of Alaska. For the present the family of three had lost sight of the others.

They passed through the Strait without being killed by the Eskimos, who could sit in the doors of their igloos on Little Diomede Island and shoot the walrus as they went by. Beyond the Strait the family's floe, however, drifted into a fleet of white-men's whaling vessels. The ships were waiting there till the arctic ice should withdraw far enough so that they could proceed up the coast in their search for whales, and they were filling their time by taking some walrus—sea-horses, they called them. Walrus blubber yielded only a little oil, enough to salvage, but the prize was the ivory of the tusks.

A small boat put out from one of the ships. As it approached the floe, the three walrus dived. The little one rode on his mother's back, grasping her neck with his flippers. They were safe in the depths of the water, but frequently they must breathe. It was an unfortunate walrus habit to swim in a straight line, not maneuvering to deceive the men, as a seal or a whale might have done. By following long enough, therefore, the men had been able to make a sure strike.

The one they killed was the mother. She was swimming then with her young one clasped to her breast in her foreflippers; she was shielding him even while shot after shot was striking her. He was bewildered to have her embrace relax suddenly, and he followed the boat as it was towing her body back to the ship. At the vessel a cable was fastened around her chest and her body was hoisted on board. He must stay with her, he must climb up to her, that he knew. He tried to work his way up the side of the ship, groping against the hull with his flippers. The sailors did not want to kill him, for he would be of no value to them, but one thought of something amusing—they would take him on board for a while. He too was hoisted up.

On the deck was his mother. She lay there, curiously inert, but surely soon she would make some sign. He crawled onto her back, as he had so often done, and patted her sides with his flippers. His breath was coming in short gasping sobs. The men stood in a circle around him. They did not all laugh. One said,

"Oh, come on, let's put him back in the water."

The young walrus was thrown overboard. He swam to his ice floe and there found his father, who would have tried to defend his family if he had not become lost from them. The two proceeded to more-distant ice, where they were out of the men's sight, and safe.

For a few hours the young walrus' only problem was loneliness for his mother. Then he began to be hungry. When his father dived to the ocean floor for a meal of clams, the little one would go down with him, but he himself had no means of getting that food. His discomfort increased. For three days he moaned and cried plaintively, finally staying most of the time out on the ice. The next morning a small seal climbed out of the water beside him. It did not fear walrus; they did not attack seals, at least not if their normal nourishment were available. But the young walrus was starved. He was several times the size of the seal, and had several times its strength. He killed it, and tore off its skin, and although he did not quite relish its flesh, he ate it.

In the ocean were many seal infants whose mothers had already left them, for the seals, living on shrimps and fish, early learned to take care of themselves. The walrus caught others, although his hunting became more difficult when he began to have the revealing scent of a flesh-eater. It was an odor the seals quickly recognized and took flight from.

By the time that he and his father had found the herd again, the other walrus detected the change in him. The mothers particularly, with their own young to protect, would drive him away. He stayed farther and farther out on the edge of the herd as the summer advanced. When the rest of them left for the south on the drifting ice, he was not with them. He did not know of their going, nor did he follow. He had become an outcast before he was six months old, a rogue walrus, as men would call him, one of those who ate and acquired a taste for warm-blooded animals rather than shellfish, because their mothers were captured before the digging implements of the young had matured.

At all times there were a few such rogues in the arctic. Every hunter could recognize them. On their rich fare they grew larger than other walrus, and they also could be identified by their tusks which, being used for an abnormal purpose, remained short and were pushed out on a sidewise slant, no doubt from the rogues' efforts to get their mouths into their meat. Their temperaments were ferocious, inasmuch as they lived by killing. Some Eskimos, indeed, never attempted to take a rogue; they were too apt to attack.

In spite of the meanness that he had developed, the rogue now near the end of his life span had never ceased to long for the companionship of his kind. Each summer he went from his wintering ground near Wrangel Island to spend a few weeks on the outskirts of the walrus congregation at the clam beds off Icy Cape. Still pursuing his hunt for seals, he would be in sight of the herd. He could hear them sing, hear their deep and resonant chorus. When the wind was right, he could get their scent, the scent especially of the females. He never had known a female, though in other circumstances he probably would have been a mate faithful through life.

That herd which came north did not include any walrus as old as he. It was the custom that after their vigorous years were over, the walrus remained on the small Punuk Islands,

southeast of St. Lawrence Island, a southern resort with pro-
lific clam beds offshore and a climate mild for the North. On
the Punuks the ancient ones foraged and swam together and
loafed on the beach, lying in such a close pack that one could
not lower his head without jabbing into his neighbor's hide
with his tusks. They grumbled and bickered a little, but the
arrangement was in fact sociable, safe, and easy—as pleasant
an old age as animals anywhere knew. The rogue should have
been sharing it. That last deprivation was the final debt that
men owed him. If the event in his infancy did not remain in
his memory as a clear picture, yet the sailors' treatment of him
and his mother, their association with a dreadful and shocking
experience, had touched off a hatred of men that later inci-
dents had confirmed. So many years of misery he had known—
and now on this June day one of the human beings that were
responsible for his suffering could, any time that he wished, be
his victim.

The Eskimo on the ice raft had got to his feet. He was
holding the harpoon aloft in his hand while his feet, wide
apart, were braced against knobs in the ice. Tiny creature: he
weighed less than a tenth as much as the walrus, but his face
and his movements showed guile like that of an arctic fox,
an animal that the walrus knew but had never been able to
catch. Courageous and poised, the man waited.

The walrus lowered himself in the water and blew out his
breath just below the surface, causing a shower of spray. He
came up again, water dripping from tusks and the bush of
bristles upon his lip, and he flung his head back and bellowed
again his horrendous threat. His prominent eyes looked red,
actually from the eyeshine which helped him to see when he
was submerged, but they appeared bathed in blood to the man,

who turned his own eyes away from the fearsome sight. The walrus detected his weakening, and his roars became louder. It did not lessen his anger to smell the dead seal and see the man, as he appeared, guarding that meat.

Each time the walrus dived under the surface the impulse to upset the ice pan took shadowy form; yet each time he rose again and repeated his menacing show of anger. He was greatly enjoying this contest. It gave him a flash of pleasure to see the man lower the harpoon, now, in his tired arm, later to see him drop to his knees, to pass his hand over his eyes in a gesture of dizzy fatigue. By such stages the walrus was conquering.

Meanwhile he too was becoming a little tired. If his strength was not what it once was, his capacity for strong feeling also, for passionate wrath, appeared to have dimmed. The fearful and bloody mauling that would have given him utmost satisfaction a few years earlier began to seem slightly arduous, like climbing upon a high ice cake, like the swim under the corridor of conflicting currents north of the Bering Strait, which he would soon undertake. Now there were moments, from time to time, when the smell of the seal on the ice was more provocative than the man's helplessness.

Late in the evening a wide quietness spread across the sea. The birds, the auklets, paroquets, murres, and cormorants, which had been canting by, all had disappeared. The fulmars and gulls were perching about on the ice, sleepily. Although the sun stayed above the horizon, the beautiful arctic night drew a brief opalescent shadow from east to west. It passed, and the sun's circular path tipped higher: another shimmering day had commenced. The walrus continued to swim back and forth in the lead.

The Eskimo had been under an almost intolerable strain for fifteen hours. He was still able to think however. He was indeed as smart as a fox, for he had planned a stratagem to be used at any minute the walrus' anger seemed to approach a climax, or otherwise when he had tired enough so that food would appeal to him more than carnage.

The man stood up and tied the paddle to his harpoon again. Now he was ready. The next time the walrus swam to the wider end of the lead, the man picked up the small seal and heaved it off to the side of the ice pan. It fell with a splash, and the walrus stopped. Startled, he hung at the surface. The seal was sinking—food for his taking at last. He lowered his head, and the arc of his great back and finally his hind flippers came out of the water as he rolled down in a dive. Ahead in the transparent depths was the silvery seal, dropping flatly and slowly, so slowly that even one weary with age could not fail to catch up with it.

Closing his foreflippers around it, clasping it as a mother would carry her young, the rogue had only one wish then, to escape with his prize. Staying close to the ocean floor, he swam northward, away from the man who had so long denied him this nourishment. The scoops of the Eskimo's paddle were audible from behind, but they only quickened the walrus' urge to hasten away with the meat, out of the reach of the man's harpoon. For a distance of several miles the walrus rose only to breathe, submerging again at once, continuing on his journey, which had become a flight now. When for a space of time he had heard no more of the Eskimo's sounds, he hooked his tusks over the edge of a floe, pulled himself high enough so he could put the seal up on the ice and, grasping the brink with a flipper, heaved himself to the surface.

While he was eating the seal, he knew only the satisfaction of having his hunger stilled. Finally all of the meat was consumed, only the larger bones and the hide remained. The walrus stretched out on the ice and dozed. But he was not quite at peace. A consuming, intense emotion had passed from his hold, had scattered. An enemy that he might have destroyed was alive, was unharmed. A man, killer of walrus, could have been his victim, but he had not acted.

When the walrus awoke he dived into the water. Now he would start for the coast of Alaska. He swung through the sea at a leisurely speed and soon was able to hear the grinding of ice along the midline of the contrary currents above the Strait. Like parallel rivers, bound in opposing directions, the two streams in the ocean passed and, since each was bearing a load of ice, the ice churned in an unearthly, screeching and crashing chaos. Cakes, blocks, and pans of every dimension from boulder to cabin size tumbled together, a monstrous tumult. Off at the sides the disturbance gradually diminished, but a strip in the center, miles in width, could only be crossed by staying well under the surface.

The confusion itself was a challenge, and coming up for a breath in that turbulence was impossible. Any animal that encountered such ice would be instantly crushed. But the walrus had made this trip many times—why did he now hesitate? For half a day he swam back and forth, seeming to dread the test of his strength and endurance. His delay was only a proof that the time comes when every creature can no longer surmount the hazards of his environment. With a new morning, however, there was a rise in the walrus' vitality, and his daring rose with it.

He moved toward the heaving ice, at the edge took several

quick deep breaths, and dived. Brushing along the sea's pebbly floor, he swam at his fastest pace into the turmoil. Soon he was under a ceiling of rapidly shifting, luminous, crystal surfaces, out of which geysers of bubbles kept spurting down. Often a jolted ice cake would hurtle below, and the rogue must dodge.

The clamor, as with all sounds, was magnified in the water. It soon had exhausted the walrus' nerves, and he was swept into panic. It made his need for a new breath seem desperate. Yet he continued on, since he must. Finally an upward glance showed that the ice was more tranquil. Still farther, and spaces of quiet water opened between the cakes. Relaxing a little, the rogue found that he was not suffocating. He stayed in the depths for more than another mile; then he came to the top, filled his lungs with air, and looked over the limpid water, strewn with scintillating and placidly propelled floes. He had entered the sea of his summer wanderings after an ordeal which, this time, had seemed unendurable. Never again would he return to his winter grounds off the coast of Siberia.

He climbed on an ice pan which the current was bearing, with other floes, toward Icy Cape. Two days passed, during which the rogue's wish to join the walrus herd he would find ahead became uppermost in his mind. His longing was strong enough to be blurring his knowledge that he was offensive to them. They would stay off the Cape for a month, there where the mussels and clams on the ocean floor were so numerous that a walrus could dig up a bushel of them, as much as his stomach would hold, as fast as they could be swallowed. Icy Cape was the chief summer stop for the herd. They would later go on to Point Barrow, Alaska's farthest-north tip, then offshore and at the season's end, would swing to the west, catching the southbound current down the Siberian side of the Bering Strait.

The permanent arctic ice pack stood twenty miles out from the shore when the rogue approached Icy Cape. As the current had brought up the floes of migrating ice, these had jammed up against the pack, and many more were arriving. Small pans and cakes like the rogue's, they were scattered over the surface, all slowly and tranquilly drifting. The time was late afternoon and the sun, dropping down toward the ice, touched it with incandescence, so that great burning coals appeared to be scattered over the water. Except for the current's deep flow, the water was nearly still. No breeze rippled it; the swells were but shadows, blue bands gliding over the silver gloss of the sea.

It was a scene that seemed waiting for music, and soon the rogue did hear singing, the droning hum of the herd's chorus, rich and clear and as sweet as a call. He was stirred with an old and forgotten impulse, to make sounds like theirs. He tried; but his voice, accustomed only to roar out threats, proved too hoarse and uncertain for gentler meanings. After a few melancholy grunts he gave up the attempt.

And then the herd came in sight. They lay on the edge of the ice field, thousands of massive brown bodies, a ridge of color unbroken and regular as a mud bank. Now too their scent was reaching him. It was the mild odor of animal flesh that is nourished on bland-flavored foods such as shellfish or plants. Almost a year had passed since the rogue had been able to smell it.

His ice pan was not moving fast enough. He dived into the water and, with only a little doubt, began making his way toward the multitude. Part of his hesitation was due to another odor, the human scent, that he was detecting faintly. It came possibly from an Eskimo camp on shore. A land smell was in the air though the coast, off to the south, was too far away to be seen.

Some of the herd had discovered the rogue. Their tusks, a row of white spears, had lifted. And the tone of the chorus had roughened. Into the song came a warning, the *huk, huk, huk* of annoyance.

The rogue remained close to the surface, rising often to sense the herd's nearness. Ahead of him more than the tusks had reared. Most of the walrus were sitting up, swaying their heads back and forth.

With a crash, followed by dazzling pain, a bullet had struck the skull of the rogue. It entered through one of his eye-sockets. With his other eye he could see an Eskimo boat dart out from behind an ice cake. Three men were in it. One was standing. All were aiming their guns.

It was hard to tell which was swamping his head, blood or fury. Blinded by one or both, he plunged toward the men: men, hated always . . . men who would block his wish for much more, now, than a seal . . . men who this time had killed him.

A dozen more bullets had struck his hide, but he did not submerge. He drove on.

He had reached the boat. He heaved himself out of the water, hooked his tusks over the side, and bore down upon it with all of his weight. But two of the men, grasping his tusks, tipped the boat out from under them. Diving beneath the boat, the rogue threw up his tusks and then drove them into its walrus-skin cover. He ripped the hide from one side of the boat to the other and shattered its framework. He continued to tear it, to mangle it, until nothing was left but splinters of wood and tatters of hide sinking down to the floor of the sea.

Where were the men? The walrus swung back to the surface. Two of the Eskimos had already got themselves onto the ice; they were helping the third man to climb up the edge. With all the living left in him now the rogue would upset that cake. Then he would treat the men as he had the boat. He would thrust his great bulk up under the floe . . . in a moment when he had recovered . . . a moment . . .

The darkness came quickly over his mind, as he was feeling the water fold up from beneath to enclose him, as it was taking him down slowly into its clean, cold, inaccessible depths.

There he might lie forever. But if his body did float to the surface, the Eskimos could not have it. For they had not saved their paddle, nor guns. They did not have any means of propelling their ice cake. They stood on the ice, now nakedly helpless, at the wind's mercy. It could take them to shore in a few hours' time or it could blow all the floes and the permanent pack farther away from land, toward the North Pole.

Men were the ones who had caused the loneliness of the rogue's life, and men had ended it, in the only way it could be dispelled. Three of those humans, for all that they had one another's company, would discover loneliness too, on their small raft of ice, adrift under the fresh, tender blue of the wide arctic sky.

CHAPTER 9

The Brave Fawns

It was late in the morning, an arctic day of fine, sunlit clarity, when the Eskimos' walrus-hide boat pushed its prow into the beach south of Icy Cape. The trip down the coast from the family's cabin at Barrow had taken almost a week. Part of the way they had wound between glittering floes of the offshore ice. If it had packed in tight, the ice would have stopped them, but everywhere they found open leads—a promising start for their expedition.

In the big *umiak* were the camping equipment and drums of gasoline for the outboard motor. When they returned it was hoped that the boat would be filled with a winter's supply of food—walrus meat, fish, and possibly caribou. Strenuous work awaited the men, somewhat hazardous work since they would be hunting walrus. Sometimes the whole herd attacked, or a single enraged animal seemed to gain strength with each wound; but risks had their own appeal. The men, as well as the boy and girl, felt that the summer ahead was a hoard of pleasure, a hoard from which they would draw daily portions as, during the months to follow, they would little by little consume the food.

Here the ice pack had drifted away, out of sight, but the ice blink, a reflected shimmering band, was visible like a halo above the horizon. Winter was permanent out on the ice. On the land however the new, brief, lovely season had come. The land, the tundra, was flat as the sea, with no tree or bush lifting above it. Only a few weeks earlier the whole arctic plain, hundreds of miles of it, had been blankly white. On that day it was green and over it hung the fragrance of earth and of growing grass, moss, lichens, heather and sage, and of small brilliant flowers. If the wind should rise and blow shoreward across the ice, the air would be chill, but now it was warm, a limpid and buoyant freshness.

In it the boy and girl and the men moved like swimmers who take delight in the feel of the water. They had discarded their parkas; at last they could sense the touch of air on their skin, after the winter when clothing of caribou hides had been needed for insulation. Even if they had been staying at Barrow they would have closed up their cabin and moved into a tent, shedding the walls as they shed the parkas, to be out of doors, every moment to smell the flowers, to hear the waves so long silenced by ice, to see the sparkle across the blue surface, after the months of darkness to live in light.

As soon as the children jumped down from the prow of the boat they set out to find favorite remembered spots from the previous year. They played until after midnight. Meanwhile the men put the camp in order. The gill net was strung out from shore on its line of floats; already one catch of fish had been hauled up and laid to dry on the new rack of driftwood.

The four dogs were tied each to its separate stake, the tent was toggled down firmly enough to withstand any wind, and the sheet-iron stove had been set at the entrance. Finally, when the sun had climbed high on its path of another day, the children crept into their caribou sleeping bags. Soon the men too went to bed. They were not disturbed by the sunshine that brightened the canvas above their heads. There had been no full darkness since April and now, two months later, their sleeping had lost all relation to night and day.

When the men awoke it was nearly noon. The children had not yet stirred. The men drifted up into consciousness at about the same time; perhaps the same sound had roused them. It was a chorus of singing voices, which came to them over the sea from the north.

"Those voices are like guitars," said one of the younger men. He had guitar records for his phonograph in the cabin at Barrow.

"I do not think so. I think they are like bells," said the eldest brother, the children's father.

"What kind of bells?"

"Church at Barrow," Ningeok answered.

The men got up almost at once and pulled on their waterproof sealskin boots and again their parkas. Over the parkas went white drill snow-shirts, which would help to disguise the men on the ice. For the voices they heard were those of the walrus, here again after their winter migration down to the Bering Sea. The walrus would be on the offshore ice, under the blink. When they had finished breakfast the men would go out for the first day's hunting.

They did not talk. No one said, "Well—so they've already come," or "We'd better get started before the wind rises," or anything else to destroy the silence. Silence was like the sunshine, a benign atmosphere in which a man's mind took its ease. Besides, they knew the procedure as surely as did a family of wolves that required no words to agree on which would herd caribou from one side and which from the other. The men carried supplies to the beach: cans of gasoline, cartridges, Ningeok's harpoon with its long line and inflated sealskin to trail an animal they might only wound; also tea and a Primus stove. On the ice would be fresh-water ponds, melted snow, and if they were gone for several hours tea would renew their energy. Ningeok's gun was ready. His brothers oiled theirs while Ningeok prepared breakfast. Filling the stove with driftwood, he soon had a hot salt fire over which he made pancakes and coffee. Each Eskimo took in addition some of the drying fish.

The children by then had come sleepily out of the tent. The boy, five, was named Alliak but the missionaries had renamed him Joseph. His sister, Ahkhrah, or Lolly, was nine. They wore Eskimo boots but the rest of their clothes had been chosen out of the mail-order catalogue. Joseph's were corduroys and a shirt with Hopalong Cassidy rearing up on the front of it, Lolly's a sweater over a cotton dress, blue printed with small red airplanes. Her black pigtails were fastened with rubber bands.

Both children had firm, full cheeks, ruddy under the deep-brown burn they had acquired from the sun shining on snow, and strong lips that often curved up from their teeth in quick, generous smiles. Lolly's dark eyes were shy but the boy's shared all of his thoughts, with his young uncles particularly. He sat down on the sand in front of them, watching them work on the guns.

Lolly and Joseph had noticed the voices. They caught from the men the feeling that this was good fortune, to have the walrus come only a day after they themselves had arrived, and to be so near. As soon as the meal was over the men carefully stowed their gear in the *umiak*. Their sleeping bags might be lying in heaps and the dishes might now be scattered about in the sand, but when an Eskimo set out to hunt, all his equipment was placed exactly where it would be at hand for the lucky shot or the emergency. After the men had pushed the boat into the water and waded out and climbed in, the children's father looked back and smiled. He called,

"Pick us some sorrel and willow leaves. For supper we'll have a salad and walrus meat."

Those were his only instructions. The boy and girl watched as the boat skimmed out over the water. The northern sea had its own ways of becoming a menace—through fog, a storm tide from the west, sudden winds, and the movement of ice, but on that afternoon it was oily-smooth and the men should not have any difficulty in reaching the herd, or in returning if they came back before night.

Joseph and Lolly began to explore the beach. This was play but, as often, play with a serious purpose, for something they found might help to solve the tough problem of staying alive. They missed nothing. They poked into every lemming's hole and scanned every clump of grass. Lolly examined the driftwood for any piece that might be the right shape to carve into a bowl, a root pick, or knife handle. The children looked also for wreckage, which was uncovered frequently on this shore where formerly more than a dozen whaling ships in a single year had been crushed in the ice. With a pounce Lolly snatched up a brass hinge—it would please her father. Every few moments, almost unconsciously, she was lifting her face to see whether the wind had risen.

Off the coast here were sandbars, many miles long, pushed up by the ice that kept charging against the shore in the winter. A sandspit ran out from the beach near the camp and connected with one of the bars. The children were walking along the spit. Nowhere on earth was there a wider horizon around two small figures. The distant edge of the sea circled them on one side; on the other the tundra spread back to a line equally far and level. In most years, now, only one ship came up the coast, the supply ship for Barrow, no road crossed the tundra, and the route of the bush planes seldom took them near Icy Cape. But the children were used to space; they were not lonely. Motionless puffy white clouds were lying just over the ice blink. Except for the clouds and birds the great sky was empty of everything but the sun and the exquisite silken-blue color, so filled with light.

The top of the sandspit was furrowed with little ridges. Between them were ponds and in one a bird like a tiny duck, a red phalarope, spun around at a dizzy pace trying to stir up insects. Lolly said,

"Maybe that apa have nest. We'll find it and eat his eggs."

"If he has eggs, he is not apa. He is ama," said Joseph. But Lolly informed him,

"That ama bird does not stay on her nest. When she comes in the spring she is just like a man. She chase apa bird, she make loves to him. If he says yes, she lays eggs in the nest, then she goes away. Apa sits on the eggs and when birds come out of them, he is the one that feeds them. But maybe they are not out yet." Her fingers searched through the grass. Joseph said,

"Our apa is like that bird. He takes care of us."

"It is not the same," answered Lolly. "If our ama was not in the cemetery she would be with us here."

Besides Lolly and Joseph many small creatures were on the beach. A flock of arctic terns rested and preened just above the line where the swells came in and broke with a sound like the thudding of padded feet. A float of slate-headed Sabine gulls rode the swells, sandpipers trotted on spindly toes up and down the wet sand, and overhead other birds were calling as they passed constantly from their inland nests out to the edge of the ice or to patches of krill. Dragonflies and bees darted and hovered above the grass and a snowy owl hawked along the sandspit. As he approached the children his eyes peered into theirs from out of his round sober face. Lolly felt a slight prickle of fear, but she destroyed it by saying,

"Apa will shoot that owl." She was sure that he would, for owls were delicious.

She continued to hunt until she had found the phalarope's nest. Four eggs were in it. The children broke open the shells with their teeth and sucked out the contents, ripe and strong. They tried to find more.

Joseph discovered a little trail in the grass, followed it and soon captured a lemming. It was a long-furred midget, mouse-size but shaped like a marmot. He put it into his pocket and every time that he felt it squirming he loved it the more. It would be his pet. The children went back to the camp, dumped out a wooden chest full of food from home, flour and sugar, coffee and tea, and put in the lemming.

"It came from a star," said Lolly. She had the Eskimo child's wish to be sharing everything, not excluding her knowledge. "One time Ama caught one. She was looking up in the sky

HENRY
BUGBEE
KANE

and she saw this kay-lung-meu-tuk come falling down. He landed right by her foot. She killed him and cut him open. It was winter, but his stomach was filled with green grass. It was very fine grass, like hair. That grass does not grow here. The mouse ate it up on his star."

"We will not kill my mouse," Joseph said. He had heard all his life that lemmings fell down from the sky and he did not need to see what was in its stomach.

Watching his pet, he dropped off to sleep. Lolly cleared up the disorder from breakfast and stacked the food from the chest in a folded tarpaulin. Then she ate a piece of the drying fish and threw one of the fish to each of the dogs. She did not go near them since they were not always safe, but it was late afternoon, time when they should be fed. There were only fish enough for another day and she went down and looked at the gill net. She saw the flash of a salmon, trying to loosen itself from one of the meshes, and a flounder already still and dead. The water was deep; they would have to stay in the net till her father and uncles were here with the boat. As she

walked to the tent again she could feel a fresh breeze on her face, and she turned and looked over the sea. Waves had risen. She wished that her father would come. She and Joseph had not yet gathered the sorrel and willow leaves. Near the tent was the mouth of a creek that flowed to the sea through a small ravine. The gully was choked with dwarf willow brush. And Lolly knew where the sorrel grew, on the tundra above the banks. She woke up her brother.

The next morning the men's sleeping bags were smooth, just as Lolly had spread them out when she went to bed. She lay quietly until Joseph opened his eyes. At once he said,

"I do not hear the walrus."

"You hear the wind. But it is not a very big wind."

Joseph contributed his own bit of courage:

"I think they come back tonight. Maybe they catch lots of walrus."

Outside the tent the children looked over the empty beach.

"Do you want a fish?" Lolly asked.

"I want pancakes."

Together they made the fire, and Lolly stirred up some water and pancake mix. She opened a can of milk and gave Joseph a cupful.

She already had planned the day. A few miles up the coast a flock of terns had their rookery. There would be a supply of eggs, large and nourishing, and for an emergency more than eggs. She and Joseph set off at the top of the mud bank above the beach. Both children kept looking out over the unbroken plain of the sea but only Lolly, perhaps, had observed that the ice blink was gone. With that discovery the need for food became pressing. It was an urge that was more than a thought; it was a restlessness in her very hands, in her knees as she walked along.

When they were still more than a mile from the rookery she suggested that Joseph should wait for her there. She would spare him the hunt, since he was so little and tender-hearted. She went on alone toward the stir of white wings. As she drew near the nests, the terns swept out over the sea in a panic but soon they were back, wheeling and screaming above her. They would dart down till their pointed red beaks were an inch from her head, and she kept up one arm to protect her eyes while she searched. About half the nests contained eggs, two in each. Around those that were empty young chicks were scampering into hiding places beneath the grass. Lolly took one more look out across the sea where the sky's blue now met the water so sharply. Then she caught one of the chicks and without giving herself time to shudder, twisted its neck. Another, another, all she could find she killed. Next she fastened her belt tight around her waist and gathering the eggs, slid them carefully down the neck of her dress.

Joseph was more unconcerned than she had expected about her armload; he took some of the dead chicks and carried them. The children walked back more slowly, Lolly being so bloated with fragile eggs and both of them tired. The sun was well into its swing downward along the north.

As they approached the camp Joseph, without speaking, pointed across the tundra. Up out of the willows along the creek a great light beast had appeared—a white wolf, larger even than Lolly. It had stopped and stood motionless, watching them. Lolly said,

"Don't let him know we see him." They went on, not

showing they wanted to hurry. From time to time Lolly glanced at the wolf. She told Joseph,

"He won't attack us—he isn't wagging his tail." Soon she saw the wolf start to lope away with his rolling gallop, his head going down when his front feet struck the ground and then coming up with them, not with a bounce however; there was no joy in his motions, rather a look of sullen aloofness. Lolly thought that he probably smelled the tern chicks and she wondered whether it would be safer to drop them. Maybe not, inasmuch as the wolf seemed to be turning away.

When the children came to the camp they found that the wolf had been there. He had not touched the fish—had he left because Lolly and Joseph had come into sight? He had torn open most of the boxes of pancake flour and both bags of sugar. The sand in front of the tent was as white as snow. Lolly threw all of the chicks to the dogs.

A few hours later Joseph was in his sleeping bag in the tent and Lolly sat in the entrance sewing a lacing on one of her *mukluks*, when the dogs began yelping frantically. Lolly's eyes looked for reassurance out over the sea, but it still was vacant. The wolf walked from behind the tent and slowly, insolently at ease, went to the fish rack. He was very near. Lolly could see his cold yellow eyes, even the black hairs in the long white ruff that stood up from his powerful shoulders.

In a breathless voice Joseph asked,

"Why are the dogs hollering?"

"Maybe they smell a ptarmigan."

"Maybe they smell the wolf. Has the wolf come?"

Lolly carefully pushed in her needle.

"I do not see him."

She could hear the wolf jump. He was pulling the fish off

the rack. Now he had them all down. He ate two, standing with one immense paw on the fish while he tore it in pieces and swallowed it. Then he took the other three fish in his mouth and trotted away out of sight up the creek. Lolly said,

"We shut up the tent tonight. Maybe you go to sleep quicker that way." She tied the flap and without undressing crawled deep in her caribou bag, so that her head was covered.

During the next few days the children stayed close to camp. They did not see the wolf, though a few times they heard him baying; they heard the voices of more than one, and the second morning they found a trail of great footprints leading down over the beach to the end of the gill net.

The net was loaded by now with fish. The children tried pulling it up on shore, but the stone to which its far end was anchored could not be moved. There still was food in the camp. A box of pancake flour was left, some cans of milk, and a sealskin poke full of seal oil. Yet hunger nagged at the children constantly, at their minds more than their stomachs. Lolly suggested that they should go up on the tundra and search for eggs.

The warm wind from the south still blew, a fitful wind whirling in quick little gusts. Now it had drawn away, now it came stinging back like a whip. The earth took it quietly. Here were no trees to sway; the grasses twitched but the tundra was otherwise motionless under the restless wind. The sky was scratched with pencilings of high clouds.

The children set out—and found that a herd of caribou had come down to the coast. It was the caribou, probably, that had brought the wolves. The wild reindeer were browsing about the banks of the creek, enjoying the young willow leaves that furnished a change from their winter diet of lichens. Their proud antlers, now almost grown, were still in the velvet. Tufts of the long, pale winter coats clung to the shorter brown fur of the summer hides; within a few days the hides would be prime for boots, parkas, and sleeping bags. The herd must have numbered a hundred or more, including a dozen fawns.

The children stood watching the animals, hesitating to move. If the men were here with their guns, what a feast they would have, of caribou tongues and boiled heads, and what an industrious time, cutting the meat in thin strips and drying it over the driftwood rack. Lolly would have been helping to scrape the flesh from the hides. It was chiefly for walrus that the family had made this trip, but they also had hoped that sometime during the summer a caribou herd would wander along within gun shot. Should the children still follow their plan to go out on the tundra? As soon as the caribou saw them they would be sure to leave.

It was a hard decision. With each day that passed there was less chance that the men would come back. Lolly well understood that she and Joseph must start to think of the ways they might feed themselves permanently. Over the tundra were hundreds, possibly thousands, of birds' nests. All of the eggs would be hatched in the next week or two. Many young birds were out, some were learning to fly. Once on the wing they could not be caught. The children would dig *masu* roots, later would gather moss berries and wild cranberries. Birds, roots and berries—they seemed like a small store when Lolly remembered the walrus meat, the great quantities of dried fish, and ducks and geese with which her family usually had begun a winter.

She had been wishing she knew how many days there would be from now till the birds would come back at the start of another summer. In getting their food together then, she and Joseph could make separate piles and see if they had one for every day. They also would need to collect a large heap of driftwood before the snow covered it. She had thought of the months when the sun would not rise. They did not have a lamp here. They could bring the stove into the tent, they would have to do that for warmth, but— When she reached that point Lolly stopped thinking about the winter.

Sixty miles up the coast was a village, Wainwright, but they could not walk to it, for a very wide river would have to be crossed. Lolly did not know where the settlements were on the other side; she thought they were farther. She and Joseph must manage to keep alive here with whatever the country provided. An Eskimo should be able to do that, she told herself.

She assumed that her father and uncles had somehow been carried away on the ice. She thought that they must have been cutting up walrus on one of the floes when the ice split up and the piece with their boat on it drifted beyond their reach. Many hunters had thus been lost on the ice off Barrow. Some had come back, more had not. Several times a day Lolly prayed for her father, sometimes praying to Jesus and other times to the tribal spirits that never were far from her mind. She had not mentioned her fears to Joseph.

It took but a moment for her to decide that they must secure the birds' eggs, even though they were certain to frighten away the caribou. She and Joseph would hide in the willows along the stream and locate the nests by watching to see where the parent birds would come flying in. They walked up the creek, most of the time in the water because the bushes along the sides were a matted tangle. Several schools of fingerling trout tried to dodge away from their feet, but the children caught some of the little fish and ate them alive, snapping their backbones with their tongues as Eskimo children did everywhere.

They had not gone far when they saw, up ahead, that the willows were violently shaking. The children froze, waiting until they knew what animal might be under the leaves. The brown ear of a caribou fawn appeared momentarily. Running forward they found that the fawn was floundering in the branches. Apparently it had been up on the top of the bank and, startled perhaps by the children's voices, had tried to bound off, only to have the edge of the soil give way under its hoofs.

Lolly easily caught it. She unfastened her belt and looped it around the fawn's neck.

"Poor tuk-tun-guak"—little darling deer, Lolly murmured. She was attempting to stroke the fawn's nose but he tossed up his head in fright. His eyes were intense with fear nd astonishment and his ears were spread wide, seeming as terrified as his eyes. Lolly sent Joseph back to the tent for a rope and they tethered the fawn to the root-crown of one of the willows. Somewhere above the ravine they could hear the click in the hoofs of a caribou, the fawn's mother, they thought.

"Now I have two pets," said Joseph. Lolly agreed, although at the time she was wondering how a fawn could be killed when one had no gun—with a stick or rock? She guessed that it probably would be very hard to beat the life out of a creature so large. Would she have strength and courage enough?

Leaving the prize they had captured, the children climbed up the bank. Hidden among the willows there, they could see over the tundra. Immediately the doe caught their scent. Poised for escape, she called to the fawn with a summons half cough and half grunt. Then she was away, vanishing farther along the creek. Her alarm warned the herd; for a moment their noses were lifted to sniff the air, and they too disappeared.

The tundra lying before the children was mottled with ponds, formed when the heat of the summer sun penetrated the ice in the soil. Most of the ponds were shallow, but where anything solid and dark, such as a dead caribou, fell, the permafrost melted down and down, to bedrock, and curiously did not freeze again except over the top in winter. Those pools were "bottomless," as the Eskimos said. Most of the sheets of water were vividly colored, due to submerged algae growths: copper, turquoise, and jade, burnished whenever the wind brushed their opaque surfaces.

For all its monotony, its simplicity, the tundra provided several kinds of habitats and Lolly, and to some extent Joseph, knew which were which and where the various nests would be found. The soil had cracked into polygons, plats ten or twelve feet in diameter, due to the shrinkage which takes place in all materials that are excessively chilled. In the spaces between the plats were ice wedges several feet in depth. The tops of the wedges were melted now, the water running together in angular ditches around the plats.

The ditches and ponds were bordered with sedges where waterfowl hid their young. The plats were drier, some covered with black and white lichens and some with grass, low berry bushes, and flowers like colt's-foot, saxifrage, fleabane, and ice-buttercups. Each grouping of plants appealed to the taste of a different kind of bird, altogether so many that here within sight was one of the world's most populous nurseries. The ponds and ditches were cradles for young mosquitoes, the prey of bird parents whose chicks thrived on insects. For the nestlings that wanted sea food, the cold Arctic Ocean teemed with shellfish and barnacles in their immature swimming stages, with comb jellies, the pretty aquatic "butterflies," limacina, and the other small lives of the plankton. They were concentrated by waves and the slight northern tides into miniature marine herds, over which the gulls and ducks hovered in wheeling flocks. As soon as one bird had a beakful, he would fly back to his young with it.

Nature does not put her commands into words; therefore words could not tell how the birds knew that they would find all this nourishment if they migrated into the arctic each spring. It was perhaps enough that they had hatched here themselves—it was their homeland. A bizarre country it was, fascinating and slightly menacing to eyes accustomed to prairies and woodlands; it was the homeland of Lolly and Joseph, however, as much as the birds. The small Eskimos were but two more of nature's children, the multitude that might give this human pair a chance to survive.

A snowy owl suddenly dropped to the brink of a pond near the children. Lolly knew that its nest would be somewhere else, and she carefully watched when it rose with a clawful of fluff and flew to one of the grassy plats. She and Joseph ran out to its nest. The owl circled about their heads, the hooks on its feet extended, but it did not attack. Since the nest was empty the children beat the surrounding grass. Soon they had found the brood, six young owls, which they drove into the bend of a ditch, where they captured them. They were fairly good size, already getting their pin feathers. The children carried them back to the willows and hid themselves and commenced their observing again.

Old squaw ducks were in sight all the time, commuting between their nests and the sea. Their eggs would also have hatched, and the downies would be near a pond. The children set forth as soon as one of the ducks alighted. Seven chicks swam out onto the water. Joseph and Lolly waded in and the little birds immediately submerged. It was a large pond. The chicks came up often for air, but they were able to see where the children were and avoid them. The water was deep, over the children's knees; they got very wet. They pursued the birds for almost an hour without catching one.

Some of the other young birds proved elusive too. If they did not swim out of reach, they could flutter away faster than Joseph and Lolly could run. By late afternoon however the children had piled up, besides the owls, more than a dozen black brant, two young of a spectacled eider, and several handfuls of smaller birds, sandpipers, longspurs, and buntings. They also had eggs of jaegers, a white-fronted goose, and a loon, all cached at the bank of the stream.

They were almost ready to stop for the day. But they had been watching a pair of whistling swans come and go from their nest, which was a high, conspicuous mound on one of the plats. The eggs would be large, or the cygnets would be if they had hatched, and so, even though the nest was at least half a mile away, Lolly thought they should make that one final effort.

As they drew near, Joseph started to walk through a patch of wet grass. Suddenly, with a terrified cry, he vanished. He had stepped into a floating marsh, aquatic grass growing over the top of one of the bottomless pools. Lolly darted ahead. When Joseph went down, the grasses had closed together above him. She clutched them back, so that when he came up he rose in clear water. Stretched flat on the ground, she extended her arms. He gripped her hands and was able to scramble out. The children then crawled to a firm, dry plat where they clung to each other, weeping with shock and fright and fatigue. It was all so difficult! They would forget the swans. They would go back to the willows, collect their eggs and birds and give up for the day.

When they turned toward the creek they saw that a flock of the big burgomaster gulls were fighting over their cache. The children ran at them, screaming and waving their arms. The gulls flew off, each carrying one or more of the birds and eggs in its mouth. Only a few of the smaller nestlings and four or five eggs remained. The children gathered them up and, disheartened and hungry, turned home.

After supper they were too tired to play and sat in the door of the tent looking over the sea. It was misty, though bright. The glitter upon its surface merged into a softly lustrous white sky. Two ravens fought with demanding cries over some booty out on the sandspit. Attracted by the commotion a dozen brant circled up from the water farther along the shore and cronking melodiously settled down near the ravens.

"Ravens always sound close and geese sound a long way off," Joseph said. Flying back and forth from the tundra were many ducks, jaegers, loons, and gulls. Some passed directly over the tent, seeming to sense that no guns would be fired from this camp. They were like the fish in a gill net, in sight and yet inaccessible.

The children soon went to bed. As they lay in their sleeping bags they could hear the wolves again, baying off on the edge of the tundra. Lolly cried,

"Joe! Maybe the wolves kill the fawn! We must get him."

While they were wading once more up the stream Lolly said reassuringly,

"Those wolves are not near."

"I'm not afraid of them," answered Joseph. "I could kill them with a big stick."

The small deer was standing down in the creek when they came to him. Lolly did hope that no wolf would find them thus cornered here, for they must take their time, win the fawn's confidence or he would not go with them. They talked to him and he finally allowed them to scratch his chin.

"He is a brave little fawn," said Joseph. Lolly pulled on the rope and he walked a few jerky steps. Coaxing him, petting him, they got him eventually to camp, but he bucked when they tried to take him inside the tent. They made him a bed at the entrance out of one of their uncles' sleeping bags. Joseph opened a can of milk and set a pan of it under his nose. The fawn sniffed it but did not drink.

" It's for you," said Joseph, splashing his fingers around in the milk. The fawn reached for his hand and began to suck milk from it.

"He imagines that he is nursing," said Lolly.

"I will not eat any meat of this fawn," Joseph told her. He had guessed, then, the plan she had had in her mind. But now she was thinking that much more than one fawn would be needed to keep them alive through the winter. It had occurred to her how to measure the time: by the holidays she had learned in the white-teacher's school. There would be a long wait until Halloween, another long wait to Thanksgiving, to Christmas, to Valentine Day, and to Easter. She was realizing, after the day's discouragements, that all the birds and eggs they could find, the roots they might dig, and the fawn's meat besides would not be enough. They might as well give up hope of surviving until the birds would be back and nesting another year. They would just try to get any food that they could from one day to another, she thought. When they had nothing left, maybe Joseph would give up the fawn. To-night it did not seem very important whether he would or not.

A fine sift of dusk had fallen; already the shorter days had arrived when the midnight sun began dipping its edge in the sea. The children went into the tent. A few times they heard the fawn call its mother with a low, urgent grunt. But soon all three of the young ones had fallen asleep.

By morning a dense fog had come over the coast. The wind had changed; it was blowing toward shore and its moisture, chilled by the ice, turned to mist as soon as it reached the warm land. An onshore wind sometimes brought in the ice. If it did, would the men return? Lolly thought of that possibility, but she did not arouse Joseph's hope. For the time now was so long; the ice would have shifted into new patterns. This wind was not strong, and the sea's northbound currents might carry the ice away in the face of it. If it did come back, it would be broken in changing direction—that would be a new hazard for anyone on the floes. Lolly knew those conditions well and, being an Eskimo, she did not allow herself unrealistic dreams.

THE BRAVE FAWNS

There was no question of hunting for more birds or eggs. It was not safe to go out on the tundra in such a fog; one could be lost too easily. Joseph played with the fawn while Lolly went up the creek a short distance for some of the tiny trout and for willow leaves. She found caribou tracks near the camp and assumed that the fawn's mother had followed him and perhaps was staying above the bank.

Day after day the gray cotton walls continued to shut away everything more than a few feet beyond the tent. They imprisoned the children. Even the beach was not visible. Lolly and Joseph could find the creek but they could go nowhere else.

Seal oil and milk were the only foods they had left. Joseph was still insistent on sharing the milk with the fawn. Lolly tried to keep busy. Once she juggled some little stones, as the Eskimo girls often did at school. She had been the most skilled in her class, able to keep four pebbles up in the air at once, but she was dropping them now. Was it because she was hungry? She faced the fact that they both would be growing weaker. Then to hold off the thought she began to talk almost continuously to Joseph. They tried to remember the Eskimo legends their father had told them.

They could still hear the calls of the birds—the birds that could find their way to the sea and back to those inconspicuous nests in the fog. By now all the chicks must have passed the downy stage; most of them would be flying. Some of the voices that came through the fog were probably those of the fledglings. The sound of the splashing creek seemed to be louder than ever. It was a lively chatter, a tumbling activity, but of course it was lifeless.

One evening Joseph asked,

"Did you ever see anybody die?"

"Ama and Earnest." Earnest was an older brother that Joseph had never known. Lolly continued, "There isn't much to it. The brightness goes out of a person and then he lies still." She considered what more she should say: "The missionary thinks that you go to heaven but Apa says that the old people are right. They believe that your spirit goes into the next little baby that's born." In her mind she went over the women she knew that would soon bear children: her Aunt Ruth, her cousin Ann, and Sophie, a neighbor that Lolly especially loved.

Fatalistic like all of her race, Lolly was not frightened by anything that might happen. The Eskimos for uncounted centuries had lacked the security that most white people knew; they had shared the precarious and uncertain existence of the animals and so, even now when their life was becoming more organized, they were at ease with the great realities. As long as the children could, they would try to live, but if living were not to be possible, Lolly at least would give up without panic.

The dogs, close to starving, were listless. But one night they awakened the children by yelping. Immediately then there was a gust of stampeding feet and a blunt muffled moan. After that, silence—silence for a long time.

Finally, cautiously, Lolly went out. Behind the tent, on the sand, lay a dead doe, its throat and its tongue torn away. Because the scent from the camp still was the scent of her living fawn, the fawn's mother had stayed, and a wolf had surprised her here. The wolf, being well fed from his depredations upon the herd, had taken only the choicest parts and then apparently he had left.

"Joseph—come, see!" Lolly screamed. She was already rummaging for a knife. She would start skinning the deer. They would cut up its meat and dry it. They would have food for many more days—perhaps for the winter.

The following morning when Ningeok and his brothers came out of the fog, for an instant the children did not recognize them, so haggard they looked, and stumbling. As soon as Ningeok saw his young ones alive and well, he dropped to the ground, unable to walk a step farther.

The uncles went on to the caribou, where at once they were tearing off strips of the meat; they were gulping it raw. Ningeok crawled to the carcass. Lolly brought him a cup of milk, which he drank with lips thin and ghastly.

"Coffee," he whispered, and quickly she started to make a fire.

"Where have you been, Apa?" Joseph asked, and asked again when his father did not reply.

"On the ice, all this time," one of his uncles answered him. "A walrus attacked our boat, broke it to pieces. We got on a raft of ice and the wind carried us out. Plenty walrus there, but we'd lost our guns."

The other uncle said,

"After many days the wind blew the ice back to shore. It landed us fifteen, twenty miles down the coast. Now we're here. We get some of that caribou in our stomachs, we'll be able to go for help."

"What we worried about was you," Ningeok told the children. He smiled, wondering eyes on the deer. "Joseph and Lolly have saved us all. The children—they are the hunters."

CHAPTER 10

Love Submerged

The humpback whale lessened the swing of his tail and nosed along cautiously. There were changes here, and they might be signaling some obstruction. He did not know what he might find, for this was his first exploration up into the polar sea. The current that followed the arctic coast had been speeding his pace. It was becoming slower now, and was turning. And the whale also was warned by a slight, unfamiliar sound, a sustained silken susurrus.

He guided his course, everywhere that he went, by sounds. In the depths of the ocean where eyes were of little use, his sensitive ears could detect the curling and probing of water upon the surfaces of submerged rocks. He knew the sibilance of a flow passing a sandy bottom and moving its grains, and the liquid rustle through seaweed, different in the fronds of rubbery bladder wrack and the filaments of the lacier algae. This Northern sea was as clear as blue crystal, for few rivers poured into it with their silt, but it was not the whale's habit to trust his eyes and he therefore sharpened his ears on the sound that was hardly a sound at all, so delicate was it, and wide and continuous. Finally he ceased the pump of his tail, allowing the current's momentum to carry him. He was keeping his long flipper-arms extended, so they could help check his speed.

There it was, the new thing: a barrier that would block his path. It was not land, a coast, however; it did not extend down to the ocean floor. Its face was as smooth as the passage of water; it had in fact the same swirling patterns as water, and was translucent. The whale swung his head up to stare at it with his low-placed eyes. As he turned to the left then his skin brushed it and found it cold. He cruised for an hour along its front, and he still had not reached the end of the wall, which human beings would call an ice pack.

It was stimulating to come upon something so strange, and to let his excitement explode the whale gave a push with his tail that shot all of his fifty-foot length up into the air. When he fell back on the surface he was enclosed in a blinding white mountain of splash, but he had had time to learn that this air, too, was different—a thin nothingness like the air above other seas, yet more brilliant, filled as it was with reflected light from the ice.

He swam farther along the ice pack and came to a herd of walrus. They also were new to him—dark brown creatures, of which hundreds were down on the ocean floor digging shellfish. They were of puny size by a whale's measuring, only twelve feet long, and they looked misshapen, grotesque, to eyes accustomed to streamlined bodies of other whales, seals, and fish. As the walrus hung in the water, their tapering hind ends up and their faces against the mud, the weighty folds of the ponderous shoulders dropped toward their heads. Meanwhile the walrus' eyes watched the whale and the whale watched them, warily but with no fear on the part of either.

Both humpback and walrus had the mild manner of creatures that do not depend on combat to get their food.

The sea here was different, it was diverting enough in its way, but it was not the marvel the whale was seeking. He was searching for love, for affection, although his wish was not yet identified. Females up to this time in his life had meant mothers. That they could have other significance he would not know till he found one. In the meantime his urge kept him wandering. Being by nature inquisitive he found everything worth investigating, but his interest in the ice and the walrus did not detain him long. Since the ice had prevented his going on up the coast, he would turn back, for he would keep moving.

He was not a fast swimmer. So large that he weighed forty tons, he progressed through the water only a little faster than pygmy man walked on the shore—four to six miles an hour when there was no need to push himself, twice as fast for a while if killer whales were behind him. His ears always were tuned to detect the distinctive and threatening pulse of killer whales swimming, but there was no hint of it here and the humpback was taking his ease. In general he was traveling down the coast, but his path was a rambling one, for the ocean floor, formed of sand and mud, was as hilly as dunes. Ice had pushed up the mounds. Some of the floes of the permanent arctic pack extended down into the water as far as three hundred feet. When the winds blew them toward the shore, they pressed and nudged into the sand, forcing it upward. Only a little seaweed grew off this coast; it was too often displaced. The whale wound his way in and out of the barren hummocks. Past the cliff called Cape Lisburne, he swam through vast flocks of birds, murres, which nested upon the promontory in such multitudes that any ship which came up this route depended upon their cries to guide it around the Cape in a fog. The murres now were fishing.

After several days the whale approached Bering Strait. There he found himself stopped by a seemingly endless ridge. It was the Prince of Wales Shoal, a sandbar thirty miles long deposited by the northbound currents after they swept through the Strait, heading into the arctic. On the top of the ridge the water was only a few feet deep and the whale hesitated to try to pass over it. It was his instinct to dread any shallows, for although he breathed air, he would die if he should be stranded with much of his skin exposed. He turned to the right, seeking the end of the shoal, but before he had gone many miles he paused, his eyes caught by another astonishing sight, an oasis on this undersea desert.

There, in a space of only about the whale's own length, grew a small jungle of kelp, long, limber, olive-brown fronds of alaria, which were swaying as waves passed through them and stirred them as with a wind. Below them, like autumn leaves swept into the hollows, were sprays of bright red delessaria. The whale glided down and discovered the wrecked ship whose spongy timbers were giving a hold to the plants.

The tides had collapsed the ship, by pushing and pulling till all of the bolts had loosened. Part of the timbers were sunk in the sand, but thousands of diverse creatures had been attracted to those that were still exposed, and here they had built up a fascinating submerged community.

Through the streamers of kelp moved the shimmering forms of fish, polar cod, eel-pouts, and armored sea-poachers which peered at the whale with enormous eyes. But the really dense neighborhoods were below, on the wood, where every inch had been homesteaded by barnacles in their little lime huts, by sponges, and crimson anemones. Most of the ship's mast was covered with mussels, tied to it by their yellow elastic threads. Starfish were crouching over the mussels, humped in their efforts to pry the shells open; other mussels were being bored into by moon-snails; as soon as the snails had their holes big enough they would send in their sharp-toothed jaws and bit by bit carve up their victims. Toad crabs, disguised by the miniature marine gardens that grew on their backs, crawled about through the oasis. Shrimps and pelagic fleas darted around the edges and lugworms concealed themselves in the sand, but not in all instances well enough, for here came an eider duck swimming up to the surface with one of the fifteen-inch worms dangling from his mouth.

The ship which provided the foundation for all this life had been named *The Good Hope*. It had indeed been a good hope for these creatures, but not for the humans upon its last voyage. Built in the North, at Shaktolik, the ship had steamed up and down this coastline through several summers, but during a gale it was blown on the shoal and was lost with all of its crew and its two girl passengers. The same storm that drowned them had buried them all in unknown sandy graves.

The whale, sensing that something extraordinary was here, prodded among the timbers. Then he pushed his chin into the fronds of the kelp—and was astonished to meet the eyes of another whale, also come to examine the wreck. He confronted a humpback like himself, but wonderfully not like himself either, for this was a female.

She had seen him too. Quickly she finned, made an upward dive through the surface and then, turning straight downward, started to lobtail. Keeping the flukes of her tail in the air, she thrashed them about from one side to the other, filling the water with showers of silvered bubbles. She looked very alluring, her slate-gray and white body swaying from side to side, all encased in the air drops. Her flippers—like arms they were—spread to the sides and, turning, delicately adjusted their slant to help hold her here. The male was enchanted. He came close and with one of his own long flippers tried to caress her side.

But she was away. With a beautiful somersault she had pulled her tail down and was off toward the end of the shoal. Her flippers were out at her sides like wings while her tail, pulsing up and down, drove her forward. Its butterfly shape, twelve feet wide, was black above, white below, and as she propelled herself the white skin kept flickering, beckoning. The male followed close behind.

After she passed the ridge she turned left and swam south into Bering Strait. That was the course on which a whale's autumn travels would take him, but she was not migrating now, she was giving the male a chase. In the Strait they were down more than a hundred feet, close to the rocky bottom but avoiding its hazards by listening for the water's gurgle. Past the Strait the female swung west into the depths along the Siberian coast.

She slowed her pace here and began to examine the sea-weed, the fronds of bladder wrack that were attached to the undersea crags. From her absorption it seemed that she never before had encountered these flattened branches, bearing upon their limber lengths thousands of air-filled sacs that lifted them toward the surface. In the swifter, more broken currents she was finding the yard-wide blades of agarum, "devil's apron," a tattered plant fabric with many holes torn in it by the water's thrashing. Well, what of it—those too she must have seen many times before. All humpback whales were inquisitive, yes, but—seaweed! And even yet her curiosity did not appear to be satisfied. With the male gliding close to her all the way she had reached the wide, fan-shaped deposit brought down by a river. It was a drowned brushland of polysiphonia, whose thickets of exquisite purplish threads undulated beneath the whales as their swimming created a wave. The female was lingering over it, seeming to seek something lost, or perhaps only being provocative.

It was while they were there that the humpbacks detected the dreaded beat in the water of killer whales. At once they stopped swimming and lay on the bottom, freezing as land animals do in the hope of escaping notice. The killers were coming nearer. There must be as many as ten of them, pacing along the surface, all breaking together up through the top and then rolling down under. Now they were overhead. The male humpback was fearful for both of them, and his enormous heart started to pound. It set up a pulse in the sea; his very fright might reveal where they hid. Very loud now was the splash of the killers' dives as they sped along on their course, with matched motions. They were a little beyond the humpbacks. Rather swiftly they drew away, for their pace was fast. Slowly the humpbacks allowed themselves to float up, for they needed to breathe. When their blowholes broke out of the surface, they did not expel their full spouts of steam. They snatched only a gasp. As soon as they felt they were safer they sped toward the south, along rockier shores again, where the great tumbling of breakers would help to disguise their sounds.

It was time, surely now, for the male's beloved to want to

play. But no, it seemed that she preferred to feed. The male must be patient still, while she made a meal on the dense plankton here.

This was the season when infants of shellfish, barnacles, snails, serpent stars, and such spiny-skinned creatures as sea urchins were having their brief chance to swim around in the water freely. They would all have to settle down later into a more monotonous life on the bottom, but they were equipped at this stage to dart and dance and skim about near the surface. They were very small, many but pinhead size, but with other minute animals, like the copepods, they were the living dust of the sea and so numerous that a cubic yard of the water contained more than forty thousand of them. Tiny ferocious carnivores: in an instant then their intense little lives were over. For they were the nourishment that sustained some of the earth's largest creatures, the baleen whales.

Swimming slowly, a few feet below the top of the water, the female was keeping her head tilted up, waiting to see a thickening of the swarm that would tell her that here was the place to gulp in a bite of it. Now her jaws, ten feet long, opened wide and the folds on her throat spread apart to increase the volume within. Her admirer could see the fringes of whitish baleen that covered the roof of her mouth. Her throat contracted again and with the help of her tongue forced the water out at the sides of her lips, while the food remained, caught in the baleen's shredded fibers.

She went on for another mouthful, and while she was thus engaged the male had, at least, an opportunity for a good look at his lovable new companion. Although she was streamlined in all of her large proportions, she had the surface bumpiness that was typical of a humpback whale—the fist-sized knobs on her head, the irregular ridge on her spine, and the acorn barnacles that had attached themselves on the sides of her flippers and flukes and around her lips. The male also was crusted with barnacles. The parasites must have found something especially congenial about the skin of a humpback, for they did not grow on most other species of whales. Since they helped to identify his companion as one of the male's own kind, they may have seemed even a part of her beauty.

There could be no doubt about the attractiveness of her motions, her truly remarkable grace, the lovely way that she swam about in the buoyant element. She seemed to take conscious joy in her effortless turnings, so supple and smooth, so nearly voluptuous. The male could no longer restrain himself. He glided so close to her that his side lay against hers—but she slipped away, to the top, where she blew out her breath in a puff of steam fifteen feet high.

He could still wait if he must. Here came a school of cod. He liked cod and he liked to practice the trick he had worked out to capture them. It was the female's turn now to be the observer. Swinging upright so that he stood on his tail, he opened his mouth to its widest limits. Then he splashed with his flipper-arms, causing a noisy disturbance that frightened the fish. They must have thought that his mouth was a cavern where they would find safety, for dozens of them were fleeing into its shadowed depths. The whale closed his jaws, trapping them. One by one they moved down his gullet, which was not wide, so that they made a procession, single file from his mouth to his stomach. It was a fine display of cleverness on the part of the male and the other admitted her interest by flipping her tail.

At last she had come to the point of showing some friendliness. As they turned into the channel between the Siberian coast and St. Lawrence Island, the female allowed him to swim with his side against hers. They would stay close to the top for a while, rising in quick succession for several shallow breaths, and then they would sound, dive deeply below for as long as fifteen or twenty minutes. Preceding the dive they would break out above the surface high enough to give themselves time to fill their great lungs with air. Their heads would come up on a slant till a third of the whales' length was exposed. At that point their heads would turn down and their backs would arch out of the sea, rolling into the water again like the rims of two giant wheels. Finally their flukes would be flung aloft, would seem to hang motionless in the sun for an instant, and then would glide lower, and slip in the waves.

It was an almost vertical dive. The whales held their downward course until they were close to the floor of the sea. There they swung upward into a long, slower rise, finally back to the top for another series of surface dives. All the way they were together, their motions perfectly synchronized. It was like a dance.

South of St. Lawrence Island the whales came to a place in the sea called "the cold spot" by humans. For reasons not surely known, here was an eddy many miles wide where the waters were colder than freezing, although they did not congeal. The cold stung the skin of the whales and was pleasant and stimulating, since under their skin was a layer of fibrous blubber, a foot thick over some parts of their bodies.

There were crags in this part of the sea, inhibiting to a whale that wanted to concentrate on enjoyment, and so the pair swam to a bay on the island coast. It was encircled on one

side by the shore of St. Lawrence, on the other side by a string of three smaller islands, the Punuks. The Punuks were densely populated; they were a kind of Florida for the walrus now grown too old to migrate into the arctic each summer. Off one beach some of the walrus were digging clams, but the whales ignored them.

Here at last the female would play. She threw herself up in the air, fell back on her side in a cradle of splashes, rolled over, and somersaulted into a dive. Again and again she swung to the top and turned down again, rollicking plunges below, with the male close in pursuit. Every time that she came to the top he tried to be near enough for a love pat, a mighty blow with his flipper. The slap could be heard for miles. Sometimes in eluding him she would give him a brush with her flukes; then she began cuffing him in return. The tumbling became faster—the sea was churned into sudsy foam. Half the time now they were out of the water, leaping clear of it, dropping down into sunlit showers.

Would she never be still? Soon she would. She lay on her side at the surface, the male drawn up close to her, tenderly stroking her skin. She did not swing away. Her own flipper rested upon him with what seemed a caress.

Their frolic in no way had frightened the walrus, who had continued to swim back and forth from the Punuk beach to the clam beds a few hundred yards from shore. Not long after the whales became quiet, however, the walrus suddenly left the sea. In some haste they sped back to the island, hauled themselves out, and clambered up onto a ridge. The humpbacks, absorbed in a game so delightful, did not notice the walrus' leaving. They were not warned, as they might have been at another time, by this evidence of the walrus' alarm.

Nor were they aware as soon as they should have been of an ominous beat in the water. The killer whales were approaching. They had heard the great splashes, the cacophony without rhythm which could not be waves. With the humpbacks trapped as they were in the bay, the killers discarded caution. They came speeding on with their rapier fins, four to six feet high, cutting up, in and out of the surface. There were nine of them, swift, deadly enemies who had surrounded the pair before the humpbacks discovered them.

The female raced toward the shore. The killer whales did not follow her, for they never entered water so shallow that they could not hide, submerge their tall fins. She plunged ahead at a blind, heedless pace. An oncoming breaker deluded her into a sense of depth under her; when it receded she found her belly upon the beach. The stranding was dangerous in itself, but she had escaped from the killers.

The male was fighting them. They were smaller than he, but quicker and spurred by a frenzy of blood-thirst. One was tearing bites out of his tail, another was trying to pry his lips open. If the killer could get its head into the humpback's mouth, it would start eating his tongue, but so far the humpback was keeping his jaws tightly shut. The terrible teeth of the killer, interlocking and inches long, were ripping out chunks of his lips. The rest of the pack, mad with greed at the feast they anticipated, were springing up out of the water and jumping across the back of their victim. Sometimes they allowed themselves to fall down on him, on his spine. The shock of their weight striking him momentarily clouded his mind, but he was fighting with outraged fury.

He had no teeth that the killers must try to avoid, but his flippers, those arms a yard wide and five times as long, were hitting out with a force possessed by the flippers of no other kinds of whales. Already two of the killers, stunned by the blows of the flippers and flukes, drifted upon the surface inert, and one with a snapped neck was dead. The remaining six were not sportive now, they were not leaping over the humpback. They concentrated on trying to get their heads into his mouth and on biting his flukes, not`easy inasmuch as the mighty tail also was flailing. The sea was a white boiling froth, soon a pink froth as the blood of the humpback flowed from his wounds. The taste and the sight of it further excited the killers.

Most whales of the larger species gave in to panic when killers attacked them; the great blues, twice the humpback's size, would turn on their backs and allow the killers, a mouthful of flesh at a time, to destroy them. But the humpback had, in his longer flippers, a weapon that gave him a chance to defend himself. By continuing to strike out, slowly he made them give way. The victory turned on his spirit, the intensity of his will to live, and it was strong enough so that he fought till the killers became discouraged. Leaving two of their number, lifeless, behind, the pack withdrew. They swam out of the bay. The waves were dispersing the blood and the foam as the humpback lay near the surface, recovering strength, allowing the good, salty sea to bathe his raw wounds and begin their healing.

An hour passed. And then, into his wracked, weary mind, came again the thought of the female. Where was she? Toward the shore he could hear a splashing greater than that of breakers. He started in its direction.

Only the flukes of the female were in the water. All the twelve-foot length of her head and much of her body were now exposed, out on the beach. For the tide was ebbing. By her thrashing about she had hollowed a trench in the sand, in which she lay, helpless, trying weakly, futilely, to move herself back in the sea. She was panting with her exhaustion and with the heat on this cloudless day. The warm sun was beating upon her smooth, hairless skin, which was taut in its dryness. Already her temperature control had become unbalanced, since it was designed to make use of the cooling effect of a watery element. She was suffering; she had become a sick whale in these few hours of being uncovered, out in this foreign and arid world.

The male swam as near to her as he dared, but he instinctively feared that he would be stranded himself. No doubt she was hearing him, striking the surface with his wide flippers, but he could not join her, he could not stroke her, as he would have been doing if they had lain side by side on the sea and she had been needing comfort. His great sympathetic heart pulsed with his yearning, and he could not give it expression.

He did not desert the female. Even if human whale-hunters had come to attack him, he would not have left. He stayed in the bay, swimming parallel to the shore. The walrus returned to the clam beds, they who could be at home either on land or in water. There was no love play among them, since these were the aged ones; yet their freedom was, in a way, a torment to see. If only the whale too had had some means of progressing upon the shore, if only the female could get herself into the water, then they could be together; but they were separated by the impassable tideflat.

The female no longer was beating her flukes in the waves. She lay quiet until the tide turned and came in again. The water flowed over a part of her body and she revived a little and struggled as long as she felt its good touch. But it was only a shallow tide in the Bering Sea, less than two feet, not sufficient to float her nor give her the depth in which she could drive herself off the sand.

Night came, the arctic night of diminished sunlight; that was a slight relief. Before morning, moreover, a thick gray blanket of cloud pulled up out of the west. By the time that the sun would again have been hot, it was hidden. The stranded whale had a reprieve.

Her devoted friend left the bay only long enough to go farther out for a meal of plankton. He returned to the coastal waters, to swim back and forth as near to the shore as was safe. A wind, he discovered, was rising. He felt a new sway in the sea as, from the west, the wind's momentum communicated itself to the waves. Under such circumstances he ordinarily would have sought greater depths; yet he stayed. The sea was becoming murky. The walrus went up on shore.

The sky was now very dark. All was dark, the swirling water in which the whale moved, and his hopes as well. But nature, chance, destiny, was, with this storm, giving aid to the lovers. For this wind from off the Siberian coast was transporting new volumes of water eastward. A storm tide, as men called it, was rising. Already the beach on the Punuk island was narrower. The male could swim closer to shore, and the female was partly submerged.

The wind became stronger. Rain fell, rain which turned to hail and filled the sea with a deafening clatter. It flattened the waves but it did not detain the flood that was sweeping into the bay at a rate ever faster.

Wetted all over her skin by the rain and the breakers, the

female began to revive. And the wind, blowing over her moistened skin, helped to cool her. Feebly she tried a thrust of her flukes. It propelled her a little. She lay resting a few moments more, during which the water continued to rise on the beach. There came, then, a sense of its lifting her. Still it was not deep enough to allow her to turn and swim out to sea. The hail ceased, and the gusts came less frequently. The wind was diminishing. But the force that it had built up in the ocean continued to drive, even now, greater masses of water upon the coast.

The female had swung herself halfway about. She lay in the trough of the waves and was able, with one flipper out on the sand and the other pushing against the breakers, to edge herself farther around. Throwing all of her energy into a final effort she gripped the ridge of deep water as one of the larger waves reached the shore. She was free. Her flukes still were scooping out sand on their downward push, but very soon she had several fathoms beneath her. The male joined her and together they turned toward the open sea.

They passed through the cold spot, southward, seeking intuitively the Bower Bank, where a cliff on the ocean floor dropped abruptly to an abysmal depth. Over its brink they passed, the strength of the female still further restored by the freezing temperatures. They followed the steep face of the Bank downward, lower and lower, past the rocks at its base until they were close to a level bottom of fine sand and mud. Over them they could feel the welcome weight of vast layers of their own element, and they continued along in the darkness for many miles. They were sensing a sweet promise there, in the touch of each other's skin, as they swam side by side with their flukes driving in unison.

CHAPTER 11

The Bird and the Hands

It happened suddenly that the golden plover, flying along through the storm with his flock, was lost from them. In the dense nimbostratus cloud and the heavily falling snow, no one of the birds had been able to see more than two or three others. But they all felt the need to remain together and they had been keeping touch by their whistled calls. In an attempt to escape to a clearer and thinner element, then, they dropped down from the cloud layer. A uniform surface of mist was above them, but small tattered scraps of fog, fractostratus, were racing along at this low altitude. One of these maverick wraiths overtook the plover. When its dark brume had passed him, he found that the flock and their voices had vanished.

He swung upward, descended again, turned right and left, but no fan of wings took shape in the surging gray and white shadows of blowing snow. The bird's clear sweet piping became more shrill. The wind whining along the edges of his taut feathers, the snowflakes striking them, pattering like a fine, driving rain, these and the fluttering gusts filled his ears, but no other sounds. He flew more erratically as the sense of his solitude overwhelmed him. It was not only companionship that was gone. He was young, with no memories as a guide on the hazardous venture ahead, and like all the flock he had depended upon their shared instinct, the sagacity of the group. With that support missing, the single bird seemed to feel that even his physical equilibrium was upset. He was tumbling about in the air like a plover shot but not killed; he was fighting for balance.

Early that morning the flock had set out from their breeding grounds beside Bering Strait. They were all immature, about two months old, and beginning what probably was, in even the best of weather, the most perilous migration undertaken by any birds. The storm was already threatening when they left. It approached from the northwest, off the Siberian coast, and soon had caught up with them. They were over the Bering Sea, where they could not alight because of the turbulence of the waves. The urge to go on was strong, but abruptly more caution arose in their group consciousness: they would turn east toward the Alaskan shore, and when they were over land would come down and wait out the storm. The single bird, fighting his way through the fragment of mist, had failed to sense what the others were doing. When they veered toward the coast, he continued south.

By the time his own instinct told him to seek the shore, he was far enough on his way to be passing the entrance to Norton Sound. There the coast was a hundred miles east of him. Under him everywhere was the white boil of breaking waves. If he had been a diving bird, if he had had the equipment and skill to go into the depths, he could have adapted himself to the water's movement. Or had he been one of the ducks that can float and feed on the surface, his well-oiled feathers would have been able to withstand the wetting. He too could swim, but his plumage must not become waterlogged or he would be trapped on the sea, his wings useless. That would certainly be the result if he tried to take refuge down on the tumbling and seething billows.

Not finding the land he expected, again he turned west, over the Bering Sea. He came down until he was close to the water, seeking a quiet area where he could briefly alight and rest. His legs dropped from their trailing position beneath his tail for a landing, but he was warned by the scud blowing off the waves. He swung up to a higher altitude. Now however the temperature was falling, the sticky snow's moisture was freezing upon his feathers. Its weight forced him into a greater effort. Not much longer could he continue without relief.

For the first weeks of his life he had been a land bird entirely. Hatched in a shallow nest on one of the terraces of Wales Mountain, at once he had started exploring the mosses and lichens in search of his insect food. In August he changed to a diet of ripening berries, but by then he was looking with interest down on the surface of Bering Strait, on the flat, crimping expanse far below that flowed southward one day and north the next, depending upon the wind. He was maturing rapidly, he was old enough so that his parents no longer needed to cover him with their wings during storms. By the time that they left for the south with the rest of the golden plover adults, the young bird was ready to leave the mountain and spend his days on the sandspit that spread its wide shining beach from the Strait up into the Arctic Ocean.

There he fed on the small marine life, such as shrimps and

pelagic worms, that were stranded by tides. The hunt for them was diverting, requiring activity that was a slight relief from the almost unbearable tension now building up in the plover's serene and poised temperament. Of all the birds, dozens in kind and thousands in number, then gathering on that coast, the plovers were the most elegant, both in the velvet black and bright gold of their plumage and in their behavior. Like an egret or a peacock, the young male seemed a bird meant for a cultivated and parklike environment more than the prehistoric simplicity of the North's vast, ice-bordered spaces. When he had run on his long black legs to a morsel of food and neatly had picked it up, he would stand with raised head and his slender body erect, always inclined to pause, to listen, to wait. And yet in those days a restlessness often came over him. Rising into the air with his deep measured wing-beats, he soon would be flying wildly, circling, dropping, turning into near somersaults on the curves. He was driven by a new impulse, irresistible but not focused yet, not the clear command that shortly would make him ignore everything else but his southbound migration. Food would cease to have any appeal to him and the beach he had come to investigate would, in an instant, fall away from his soaring wings and away from his interest. The instinct was meanwhile maturing, just as his feathers were lengthening and his muscles becoming strong.

The bird waited—and the earth waited, for the mantle of ice and snow that before long would spread over the polar sea and the land. On the earth too an impending event was felt. The ocean no longer shone with the iridescent gloss that had polished it during the summer. Waves agitated by ceaseless winds gnawed at the beaches, waves filled with the trash they were stirring up and with the year's growth of seaweed, now pulling away from its holdfasts. On the mountain the blue crowberries and ruby cranberries were staining the slopes with a wine shade picked up by the low-lying clouds; and the end of summer was even more obvious down on the tundra behind the shore. There the cottongrass and the other sedges were copper-gold, vivid around the blue ponds that each morning were edged with ice. The winds were plucking out shreds from the fluffy tops of the cottongrass, rolling them into hanks and storing them at the roots of the stalks. In those marshes the waterfowl nests were deserted. The egg shells lay broken around the rims and the linings of down were scattered; the birds all were gone for the present year except willow ptarmigan. In their white winter coats they walked, gently alert, among the abandoned homes. Against snow they would be invisible, but their only concealment now lay in the patches of cotton and many were being caught by the hawks and owls at that time when the air was so brittle-sharp that the round, grouselike forms of the ptarmigan gleamed like white lights on the yellowing tussocks.

When he flew out above the ocean, the plover could see in its depths the shadowy bulk of the whales beginning their autumn journey. Over the shore cormorants, gulls, murres, old squaws, scoters, geese, curlews, jaegers, terns, longspurs and snow buntings, sandpipers, auklets and phalaropes and the young golden plovers wheeled and streamed through the air, exercising their wings. Every day a few strands of them would untangle themselves and draw away southward, but multitudes still remained. Most were assorting themselves into flocks. The plover joined one group of his fellows and then another, trying each company till he had found the one that was most congenial.

This homeland of his, where the dark height of Wales Mountain overlooks Bering Strait, was out on the continent's farthest tip. Fifty-three miles away was the Siberian promontory where Asia's East Cape likewise points toward another coast, that of North America. The humans did not cross the channel and most birds too, having traveled thousands of miles to this arctic breeding ground, stopped at the Strait. Siberia had its bird population that migrated south for the winter, into Japan and China, to Java, New Guinea, Australia. The birds that had reared their young in Alaska turned southeast, bound for California or inland through Canada, some to stop in the States, others to fly on to South America. Like the men who considered themselves to be aliens when separated by only the Strait, the birds seemed to find the swift narrows an impassable border—all but a few. Some of the Asiatic birds such as whimbrels and dotterels did fly over the channel to nest on Alaskan tundra, and the most adventuresome of the American birds went on to the coast of Siberia. Now those explorers were turning back; wings were shuttling between the two Capes.

The Pacific golden plovers belonged to none of these groups. While all of the other migrants chose land routes, the plovers would journey down over the Bering Sea, past the Aleutian Islands, and then on above the broad rolling wastes of the Pacific Ocean. Their goal was the Hawaiian Islands, those pinpoints upon the vast waters, which they would try to reach after a flight of two thousand miles with no sight of land. Somehow they must find their way and must find the strength to remain in the air for several nights and days.

In preparation the plover himself and the flock he had lately joined swung out from their beach in wider and wider circles. Wales Mountain had seemed an immense world, exciting and strange, when the plover was small. By now it was only one of numerous peaks there on the continent's shoulder. South of it on the Alaskan coast was the range of the York Mountains, polished and steep. From them the Eskimos once got their arrowheads, and most of the Yorks were, in fact, too flinty to give even lichens a toehold. The plover, accompanied by his band, had circled among their pinnacles. They knew how those mountains spread eastward along the wide, meandering Lopp Lagoon, which was so nearly a part of the Arctic Ocean, divided from it by flats of the wettest possible land. The plovers had many times swung past the summits, coming north again to their beach. That was only a morning's jaunt by now, and the next widening of their course took them across the Strait.

The lengthened trip was in various ways a test flight. On their migration, due to begin any day, the plover flock would progress at great altitudes. In making their expedition to the Siberian coast therefore, they rose into the layer of stratus clouds which, that morning, covered the channel between the two continents. Certain of their direction, even when they were surrounded by dense white mist, they flew west. Still they climbed, and the blur that enclosed them grew brighter. Now it was tinted with nacreous gold, and now suddenly they were above it, over a surface of fluffy down stretching away on all sides to a level horizon.

Over the stratus sheet, in places resting upon it, were altocumulus puffs, purely white billowing chimneys spaced out in the high, intense blue of the sunlit sky. Their foamy whiteness built up and up, each cloud holding together, holding its separate shape, but a shape of miraculous softness. The birds had the choice of following winding corridors bordered with luminous bosky walls, or of heading straight through the clouds. They went into the smaller ones. Darkness would thicken around them, the vapor would be a blindness, but the plovers kept calling to keep in touch and, guided well by the beacon within their nerves, they would emerge from the mist as a flock and once more progress over the loose rolling stratus floor.

The cumulus puffs ahead were drawn closer together, and then they were merging. Finally the birds could find no clear sky. Acting as one, with an impulse that generated within the whole group, they tilted their wings and relaxed their drive. Now they were down in the stratus layer again, still descending; the atmosphere merely seemed steamy, with the shadowed earth taking shape below. No sunlight was penetrating the clouds, which were quite above the birds—they were only a dull white sky.

The plovers had already flown past Siberia's East Cape; under them was a marsh with more mountains beyond, treeless slopes like the ones they knew on the Alaskan side. A river wound down through a valley, with willow brush edging its banks. The flock started to circle back. Soon they were over an Eskimo village, and bullets were stinging the air. Two of the birds were hit. They fell to the earth as though diving; one struck and bounced off an igloo roof of tight walrus skin. The flock speeded their wingbeats. They were beyond the settlement; they were crossing the shore toward the Bering Sea.

The water was wider here than the Strait. The plovers could sense the much greater demands they would have to meet over the trackless width of the Pacific Ocean. They could find their direction here too, with the sun's position not visible, with only the water below and the clouds above. Unswerving, direct was their eastward course until the cliffs of the York Mountains lifted ahead of them on the horizon.

The young male was exhilarated by the expanded flight. When he alighted upon the familiar beach, he ran about in the shallow waves with foam singing about his feet. His expedition was taking shape now in his mind; his tension was due to break in his life's most challenging venture.

It was, ironically, the imminent snow storm that would trip the flock's impulse to start. At sunset the sky had cleared above the Strait, but by morning small streaks of cirrus, white silky tufts trailing from upturned hooks, were advancing over the Northern sky. These increased and condensed into a fibrous veil hiding the sun, and meanwhile a change in the atmosphere's pressure warned of a climax in weather. The birds of all kinds were aware of it. The air was scintillating with nervous wings, though the plover flock were not flying. They perched at the top of the beach, poised to begin their migration.

Their departure was uneventful. With a common impulse they simply flew up from the shore and, ascending rapidly, turned southward over the Bering Sea. Within a few hours the blizzard had overtaken the young, inexperienced birds.

After the flock as a whole had retreated to land, the single, lost male continued above the water. By nightfall, however, he could go on no farther. Under him the great waves had increased in height. The breakers were flinging their crests off into the sky and spreading behind them coarse nets of foam, and the roar of the winds and the waters was one, a bewildering crush of sound. His will to continue was firm, but so heavy a load of ice now encased his feathers that all the energy he could put into the push of his wings would not keep him aloft.

In his descent toward the sea, he saw ahead a dark wallowing object, a small ship. It was heaved and dropped, and was battered from one side and then from the other as waves crashed upon its hull, but it was floating. The bird reached it. He circled it once and came down to alight on the rail in front of the pilot house.

Through the window behind him, blurred with a coating of snow, a man's face peered out. It was only a few feet away, yet the plover did not take alarm. To have the firm wood in the grasp of his toes was a comfort incalculable, even though sheets of spray flung themselves over him with each dip of the rail. It was enough that he need not be driving his stiff, weighted wings. He folded them, and at once they froze into place on his sides.

The ship was attempting to quarter across the waves. It had been bound from St. Lawrence to Norton Sound when it was blown off its course toward the South. The engines churned steadily, yet the breakers were rapidly overtaking it. Each time that one passed, the boat slammed down into the trough, a blow that was wracking its timbers. The face on the other side of the glass was tense, hard with anxiety.

THE BIRD AND THE HANDS

Just before darkness enveloped the scene, a door at the side of the pilot house opened. A different man, a young Eskimo sailor, came out. One hand was holding his pea jacket closed; the other hand reached for the bird. Instinctive fright seized the plover. He attempted to raise his wings; he would have flown off the boat if they had not been rigid. The man's hand closed around his body and lifted him off the rail.

Now they were in the pilot house. The captain glanced at the sailor, smiled faintly, but did not speak. The sailor went on down a narrow and pitching corridor to the galley. Two other men, the engineer and a sailor, were there, bracing themselves on benches between the cabin walls and a table, and balancing coffee cups in their hands. They too appeared sober but one, gesturing toward the stove, said,

"Look what Dummy's got. We'll have chicken for dinner."

The bird's captor, a deaf mute, caught the meaning. He grinned but he shook his head. Sliding onto a bench, he held the bird on the table before him, enclosing its frozen plumage in both his hands. The pressure of the man's fingers was like a trap; yet their warmth was welcome and the bird's heart, which had been pounding until it seemed that it would explode in his breast, subsided. With a wild creature's quick intuition he sensed that this man was his friend.

Soon the ice in his feathers had melted; now he was merely wet. When the man shifted his hold, the bird raised a wing. The sailor set the bird's feet on the rim of the table and lowered his hands to the surface, but he kept his arms spread around him to warn off the other men. The plover stood quietly, and the deaf mute began to stroke him. At the first touch, on his back, the bird took alarm. His wings fluttered, and the man understood. After that he stroked only the plover's breast. That was not a covering motion and therefore the bird did not fear it. He retired into his plover's composure and waited.

The sailor across the table again spoke:

"When the captain sees this he'll put the bird in the pot."

As if to test the prediction the engineer left, disappearing into the passageway. In a moment the captain came in, a Norwegian, a mariner with intent blue eyes that were now preoccupied; he was watching the bird as though without seeing him. The mute sailor gathered the plover into his hands, slipped him into the front of his jacket and buttoned it close. The sailor was moving; he was walking and then descending a ladder.

Down in the engine room he took out the bird and set him up on a warm overhead pipe. The bird fluttered off. He struck the dark sloping walls but at last found a perch for himself on one of the rungs of the ladder. Two more sailors were there, but they were absorbed in their work on the machinery.

The ship's violent plunging was more disturbing than any wind. When he was tossed by a gust the plover could counter the motion by his wing action, but here, though he clutched the rung, he was nearly thrown off by the shock of the hull crashing into the trough of the waves. And the air in the hold was foul with oil and bilge. Dizziness thickened the bird's mind and his head dropped down on his breast. The mute sailor had started to help the other crew members, but he noticed the bird's distress, buttoned him into his jacket again, and went up through the galley and out on the deck at the rear of the pilot house. There he put the bird down on a coil of rope. The plover was free but he made no attempt to fly.

Lashed to the deck were a dory, a snow plough, and a small pile of lumber. They were shifting and straining each time the ship lurched. The snow plough was lifting six inches or more, to bang down again on the deck, and the captain and one of the other men were now bracing it with additional tackle. The mute sailor joined them. They were all working with earnest haste, what haste they could on the tilting and wave-washed deck. In the darkness the waves and snow were lit by the beam from the galley door. After a while the men went back in the pilot house, closed the door, and the plover was left outside in the night.

Torrents of spray were slashing across the deck, and from time to time one of the breakers poured over it. The plover had little urge to take wing, for the ship, pitching about as it was, seemed less to be feared than the snow in the screaming wind. The bird made his way to a deeper niche in the coil of rope.

He was still huddling there when the black night gave way to a glowering, heavy dawn. The water could now be seen clearly, as far as the snow allowed. Its movement had changed. The storm, as often occurred on the Bering Sea, had become a revolving gale, with the wind veering so rapidly that it blew from all points of the compass in five minutes' time. The waves no longer came in advancing procession. For the sea, being shallow here, with a depth of only twelve fathoms, was quick to respond to the wind's direction. The violence had not lessened, but the surface was lifted in towering peaks without forward motion. The tossing was wild and chaotic; the slopes of great liquid summits swept skyward and sank, pushed down by adjacent peaks rising. And the speed, though so huge, was fast, seeming hungry, rapacious.

The ship had been built originally for fishermen off a coast where the weather was milder; it had neither the strength of hull nor the motive power to long stand such a buffeting. All the men's faces were apprehensive. They came often to tighten the gear that was holding the snow plough; the captain stood by it constantly. The bird and the men were sharing this danger. None could long survive if the timbers that gave them support should break up.

Noon approached, under a sky uniformly dark. Not the sun nor the wind nor the waves, only the compass screwed to its standard up in the pilot house, gave any clue to the ship's heading. Having no southerly swells to contend with now, the captain had set its course straight for the east, toward the coast, for it seemed evident that the ship would not hold together for many more hours.

The crisis came suddenly, at mid-afternoon. While the men, all but the engineer at the wheel and one sailor down in the engine room, were on deck, the snow plough broke loose. It crashed down the steep slippery deck, stopping against the rail. Its weight keeled the ship over so that the rail was submerged. If only that barrier would give way, then the plough, plunging off into the water, would let the ship right itself. But the heavy rail held.

As the ship made its sideward lurch all the men lost their footing. Two would have been washed overboard but they succeeded in catching a grip on the plough. The mute sailor had fallen against the winch, where he clung.

"Loose the dory," the captain roared. He scrambled across the lumber and reached the boat hooks. The sailor from down in the hold appeared in the cabin door. The engineer came behind him on hands and knees, his face oyster-gray with his fear. Then with a sickening roll the deck rose until it was vertical, swung on over and threw all six men into the monstrous sea.

The bird had his wings. He flew into the wind and the snow but stayed near the scene, where the ship's rusty keel hung in the water a moment or two before it slid, with a boiling and sucking above it, out of sight. The dory was riding the waves. Three of the men had gone down, the engineer one of them, but the rest could swim. The captain, reaching the dory, tossed a life jacket out to the deaf mute. One more man was staying afloat by grasping a piece of the drifting lumber.

Those three saved themselves; the captain got himself into the lifeboat and rescued the other two. They started the engine, and though the boat reeled about through the peaks and the pits of the waves, the captain attempted to steer in a circular course, hoping to find the three lost men in the wreckage that drifted upon the surface. For more than an hour the search was continued. By then all the lumber and other floating gear had been widely scattered over the sea.

The captain was scanning the sky. How, lacking a compass now, could he determine which way was east? The clouds gave him no hint, nor the sea. He was keeping the engine running, but at low speed lest he be moving away from the coast.

The bird hovered closer and closer above the boat, for the winds and the snow were still as hazardous for him as the turbulent waters were for the dory; he had wings but no motor, and once again he was much fatigued. He alighted upon the boat. Both sailors were bailing and paid slight attention to him. Once, however, so thick a shower of spray struck the bird that he was knocked from his perch and had to flutter out into the air. When he came down on the rail again, the deaf mute reached up and lifted him off and put him inside the prow, where he was sheltered.

The captain had long sailed these lonely waters, where no lighthouses, no beacons, were maintained to assist a ship, and he had been accustomed to watching the sea birds. Their actions warned him of changes in weather, and in fog their cries told of the presence of rocks and cliffs. Now a thought struck him. He said,

"If that plover would leave us he'd probably set out for land and give us our course."

He gestured to show his meaning, and the mute sailor nodded. Again he took up the plover, this time to try to persuade him to leave. He tossed him up into the air. Soon the bird was back. The sailor continued to wave him off, but the bird only sensed that out in the blowing snow was the greater danger. He would fly, allowing himself to be hurled about in the blizzard until he was tired, when he would return.

"Our gas may not last till morning," the captain said. All the men were then waving the bird away and he stayed aloft.

Dusk was thickening over the waters, dusk, night beginning to darken the white falling snow. Or was the snow thinning? The wind certainly was subsiding, and the flakes, coming down gently now, were no longer so blinding. The men in the boat were watching the plover anxiously. He could see their pale, upturned faces below him. He was sensing their interest, though he did not, of course, comprehend their actions, not hostile and yet not friendly.

The bird was immensely hungry, having been without food for all the two harrowing days. If he could reach the coast, there he could rest and feed for as much time as he needed to gain back his strength. He was discovering that his flight in this sky was becoming less perilous.

There was but little light in the sky now, and no land was in sight; yet the plover was not confused. Where the shore should be, he instinctively knew. On a sudden, decisive urge he straightened his course toward the east, away from the boat, which, as he set out, swung around so that it followed him.

Cape Romanzof, a steep promontory, took shape where intuitively the bird expected to find it. Most of the slopes were white, but with the snow drifted, as it had been by the gale, some of the terraces were but scantily covered. The clouds were blowing in tatters, were being swept out of the sky. The moon fitfully shone and its light revealed to the plover a patch of crowberries. He ate enough of the fruit to relieve his hunger before he fluffed out his feathers and closed his eyes for a long welcome sleep.

Winter had come to the North but it still was a season of only moderate cold and the sun, although sinking lower, rose every day. Its warmth melted the snow off more of the berries. The bird feasted and slept until he was ready once more to begin his migration.

He would make it alone, but he would not lose his way. On the third morning, when he set out again, a splendidly flaming sunrise was putting a wash of gold and violet over the vast white land. At first he stayed near the coast and before he had traveled far, his keen eyes discovered a camp on the beach, the well-known dory drawn up on the sand and, stretched out around a fire, the three human companions with whom he had shared his ordeal.

The sea had quieted. It was a surface on which he could

rest, should he need to stop, but the drive in his wings was a force that could carry him, so he felt, far from the arctic. He turned out over the water, south toward another coast, bordered with swaying trees and great vivid flowers, a shore very different from this, that he never had seen. There he would spend the winter. But late in the spring, when the ice and snow were due to be gone from Alaska, he would make the long flight again.

He would return many times, he but one bird in the scud of wings that every year sweep toward the arctic — the wings, the fins, the flippers, and the feet.

The Northern country is their homeland; they might never leave it if they could survive its winters. Since they cannot they come back, here to the icebound summer, for their joyous courting and the welcoming of their young. Some of them make the longest possible journey, from the continent around the South Pole. All will start from regions where they found survival practical, and on their way will pass a great variety of other habitats; nevertheless they will continue till they reach this most remote, wide, austere arctic, its cold, clear seas and skies that always are buoyant with ice-fresh winds and endless light.

They come, as well, to the worst that weather can hurl upon the planet, to tempests, blizzards, that for many will be fatal. That prospect does not stop the migrants. As they approach the high crescendo in their lives, some impulse draws them to this land of delicate loveliness and violence. Here, where storms begin, shall be the birthplace also of the most abundant life.

NOTE ON TYPE USED IN THIS BOOK

This book was set on the Linotype in Janson, a recutting made direct from the type cast from matrices made by Anton Janson some time between 1660 and 1687.

Of Janson's origin nothing is known. He may have been a relative of Justus Janson, a printer of Danish birth who practised in Leipzig from 1614 to 1635. Some time between 1657 and 1668 Anton Janson, a punch-cutter and type-founder, bought from the Leipzig printer Johann Erich Hahn the type-foundry which had formerly been a part of the printing house of M. Friedrich Lankisch. Janson's types were first shown in a specimen sheet issued at Leipzig about 1675. Janson's successor, and perhaps his son-in-law, Johann Karl Edling, issued a specimen sheet of Janson types in 1689. His heirs sold the Janson matrices in Holland to Wolffgang Dietrich Erhardt.

The book was composed by THE PLIMPTON PRESS, *Norwood, Massachusetts, and printed and bound by* KINGSPORT PRESS, INC., *Kingsport, Tennessee. The typography was based on designs by* W. A. DWIGGINS; *the binding design was by* CHARLES E. SKAGGS.